Experience Counts - How to Trade Futures, Stock, Forex, Options, With Algebra

Greed starts out by being a hobby, transitioning to a passion, then transitions to a final stage of addiction. This book talks about greed as an addiction and how a human with morals can overcome it.

Greed has ruined many Americans, and it continues to do so. Greed is the reason why millions of Americans lost their homes, it is the reason why scandals erupt, and it is the reason why we can't prosper. Greed has not only ruined the one percent but it has gone and ruined millions of selfless human beings who are out to make a decent living for themselves.

The world used to be a society filled with people not out to be better than others but to maintain their own lifestyles, today it's just a simple "keeping up with the Joneses," striving to be better than our counterparts, to be better than our neighbors and even our own family members.

This is just part of a simple lifecycle; you go to school, then college, then you get a job, retire on social security and die. Within these stages you, you slowly transition from one part of the path to the other crawling, walking, jogging, and then finally running to beat each and every single one whether it be shooting them or killing their confidence. At one point we become so self absorbed we even try to beat our closest peoples.

In the end we are so devious we kill each other like cockroaches and the ironic part is that we all end up being eaten by cockroaches. Greed is such a vital principle to human existence, but of course you could indefinitely urge that without greed we would all be hopeless ants with only one queen.

This book represents a view that is not only mine but it is prevalent in all religions from the Quran to the Torah to the Bible all religions hold a vital concept when involving greed, they all say not to be lured into the trap.

This book not only talks about greed but it then extends to include personal finance; which includes stocks, real estate, saving, and spending. This is all while maintaining a healthy and hopefully wealthy lifestyle and discouraging greed to a certain extent. Personal finance can often be the key to success, if you truly have the will to do so anyone can easily become a millionaire by the age of 40, many estimates say one must be 60 to retain his/her full wealth potential but these estimates are often leave out a vital fact.

The more you save the more you make, hence the more you can spend. Money is a vital concept and if used and estimated correctly one can become very wealthy. Although greed can't be eliminated, and most certainly can be controlled. Controlling greed is not hard it just takes some discipline.

This book features how to deal with specific circumstances in which greed can limit your earnings potential such as the stock market and real estate, and then transitions to broader topics such as family and saving.

Now enough about what this book will be about, the rest is to find out.

The Hobby

The Winners Market

Wall Street is like a game, only with a conscious, instead of being a game that has been already programmed and designed to function a certain way it is consistently being changed, manipulated, and turned to favor the already socioeconomic elite. This creates a virtually impossible way for the middle and upper-middle class to win in this game, and allows the rich to get richer and the poor to get poorer. These days looking at overall trends many people are involved in the stock market as they see a get rich quick scheme involved, what they don't see is the risk involved in it, the stock market can ruin people, but don't get me wrong it can make them rich as well, but it's just unlikely. Greed is essential in the Stock Market, because if discipline isn't there the money wont be there.

You have to remember that the fancy investors we see on TV or the eccentric billionaires we hear of buy this company and that stock did not start out that way, they started from the bottom of the food chain, with of course the exception of a few people, but the point is many investors did not become rich through the stock market but instead through their specific company. As an example take Warren Buffett although he is widely accepted to be a stock market guru, he actually started buying companies very early on, his current company Berkshire Hathaway owns many entities, that was how he got rich, by controlling the company, not speculating. Now this does not mean that average Joe's always lose but there is a good chance that they might.

This creates an unfair advantage for the majority of us who aren't that rich and don't have disposable resources at our finger tips. Just think of it as this, many of this year's billionaires attended an Ivy League school, are business professionals, and are or have been wealthy to begin with, here are a few examples Carl Icahn, attended Princeton University, was born into a Jewish family, and has been fairly rich from the start, Warren Buffett a billionaire who attended Columbia University, and Donald Trump, a billionaire who went to the Wharton School of Business at the University of Pennsylvania, whose father had given him $25 million to start his empire. There are many more examples but all of these names that are mentioned above have some stake in the stock market and whenever they buy into a company, the company generally tends to soar on the day of the announcement. These statements do don't in any way what so ever reflect any views on the people themselves, but this is just a simplistic general observation. Now for the technology sector, Bill Gates attended Harvard, then dropped out and received an honorary degree he was born into a wealthy family, his father is a notorious capital hill lawyer while his mother a school teacher. Next is Mark Zuckerberg who again attended Harvard, then dropped out due to Facebook, his father too was a professional, a dentist to be exact. I went into such great detail to show just how petrifying it can be; the wealthy control everything in our world. And they are greedy but the difference between us and them is that they are disciplined; these guys know when to sell or to stop hedging the stock.

All of the five men mentioned above have had some if not a bunch of impact on Wall Street;

this again shows how Wall Street is manipulated. Here's an example would you rather control .0000001 percent of a company or 30 percent, the correct answer is none of the above you would want to control 51 percent if not 70 percent or 80 percent of a company, that percentage or majority shareholder control allows you to have much greater leeway in accompany so you can be manipulative so you can control the company, and so you can make and create any decision you feel is the best for your company. The percentage used above is a bit extreme but in a company similar to Apple that is probably all you could afford to buy while diversifying. Now if you control .0000001 percent of a company that leaves you with virtually no room to do anything. Yet some of us still feel that investing in a technology, financial, or healthcare stock is a "safe" investment. Let's not forget those days when either a random announcement is released or earnings of a company are due. Stocks either leap or plunge enough to make us lose our sleep. Stocks are supposed to offer certainty yet they offer uncertainty; there have even been cases were a stock has stooped down lower than 50 percent after the Food and Drug Administration did not approve the respective company's drugs.

Now let us transition back to the technology sector, as an example let's say you were playing options, which is a horrible idea, but that's completely another story, so you buy ten contracts of AAPl that you have kept for six months already, and let's say you have met your strike price and are in the money. Time flies and you are now getting closer to Apple's earnings but you still don't sell because Apple has had a good rally and every financial media outlet is screaming Apple this quarter will be Apple's finest, and that may stand true, Apple may report better than expected earnings, and the stock might initially skyrocket, but what investors don't know is the guidance they are about to offer.

Selling early is sometimes a key to success in the market; the earlier you sell the less risk there is involved and the more gains are made possible. Yet, you refuse to sell, and then the guidance is released and shares start to plummet. Guidance is often the make it or break it for a stock, it can either push the stock's price forward or let if fall back. What I am trying to say is that you should not allow yourself to be fooled so easily, and this goes without saying buy do not ever put your money in one stock or "basket" if you make this mistake once it can ruin your financial progress for your entire life.

Selling early is sometimes a key to success in the market; the earlier you sell the less risk there is involved and more gains are attained.

Most notable on this case are Carl Icahn and William Ackman were they have attacked companies heads on, Icahn tends to attack the company's management while Ackman simply states they are either scams or they have other issues. Ackman infamously shorted millions of Herbalife's shares. Unfortunately for him, those shares have gone up nearly 120 percent all-in- all he lost tens of millions; in the market today there is tons of market manipulation. The big leagues control everything.

Overall the stock market is a very bad investment if done incorrectly, but can provide staggering returns if done appropriately, even though many of the world's billionaires have made tons if money off of it; such as Warren Buffett, Carl Icahn, George Soros, and William Ackman, it will not change back when the stock market was introduced it was meant to be a bit riskier than keeping your money in the bank today you can lose half if your net worth in an hour after the closing bell, if you still haven't understood what I mean by that I will repeat it do not invest in earnings.

Relating to the whole earnings pitch, try to never keep a position overnight, unless you plan to keep the company no matter what for more than a year, doing so eliminates a ton of risk that should not be played with. You should only keep a company long-term if you have seen the growth in it; as in it has a great price to earnings ratio, a decent beta, and good revenue buildup over time. Doing this eliminates a bunch of risk on your end, because if you are skeptical about the stock in the first place if it even falls five to ten percent you will sell-out. This brings me to another point, always be confident about your stock, and stick with it.

But the points are only if you absolutely feel you must invest, if you don't need to invest elsewhere where although gains might not be guaranteed at least they are promised. And if you still have the urge to play in the stock market play with buyer sentiment if a stock is trending higher buy it and if you smell even an ounce of terror in the company sell it, many legendary investors say "buy on the dips sell on the rallies."

The dip is often a key to buyer sentiment, this dip is where shares are bought the most, and the rally is where the most shares are sold. Another important thing to remember is that there will always be opportunities. Every second every minute every hour there are countless opportunities where stocks either rise or fall, so do not and I repeat do not be greedy and buy stocks based on little or analysis.

Moving on never hand your money over to anyone, whether it is a stock broker, family, or a best friend; however, the situation becomes different when they are in need, with the exception of the stock broker of course, but as for business never hand your money over, even if the rewards are hefty and promising. Each case and situation differs but these are just some of the general guidelines.

Greed has changed the ways of many people; these same people have ripped off their own family members, their own friends and have ruined their own world, for a hefty short-term reward. This has altered the course of human existence, from the politicians to even the street magician performing or the person playing the coin game. There are many instances through the course of the world's where the passion of greed has killed the person, a few instances include, The Bernard Madoff Ponzi scam, that was called the scam of the century as he not only allegedly but reportedly stole tens of billions from people and human beings just like you and me. And the only reason why people invested with him was probably because he offered a premium of a couple of percent over the industry standard, this is what I mean by being greedy. All in all he was a human and humans make mistakes, whether it not you believe this, there are numerous example of how greed has corrupted fine specimen like you and me.

Don't get me wrong greed is a necessity to humanity, as noted above if greed had not existed I wouldn't be writing this book, and you wouldn't be reading it. Greed exists as an emotion in order to let society function. Greed as a hobby is okay, but greed as an addiction is not. And no matter how severe Greed can be disciplined in the same manner new skill sets are found.

As a young investor I have found that there will be three major recessions in my lifetime and even a depression, I refer to these cycles as the Cycles of the Economy. You see there are cycles that exist as life and death co-exist profitability and unprofitability exist as well. If you closely analyze these cycles, you will find a concurring pattern and trend. Lets explore it, first as it is today the economy is fairly decent people are buying homes, people are selling homes, interest rates start to pick up again, unemployment is at a decent level, and disposable income is a bit above average as well.

Then comes a wave where inflation skyrockets, hence prices escalate and home prices are way out of line, unemployment is very low and things are starting so seem a bit out of proportion.

Finally, in this stage, people fail to stimulate the sky high economy, and in tern failure erupts. The bubble pops and sends the economy into a recession where the unemployment rate rockets up as high as 11 percent and in a depression 15 percent.

Now of course there is much more involved then what is simply mentioned above but this was just the gist of it. But the point was if you are able to recognize these cycles and patterns you can make so much money off of other people's mistakes. Back on March 6th, 2009, share of Bank of America closed the day at $3.14 per share. And is currently trading at $17.43 per share as of March 10th, 2014. Back then shares had gone through a catastrophe after Lehman Brothers and Bear Stearns had filed for bankruptcy, fear had spread like the Bubonic plague. Since that time shares have recovered but are no where near the all time highs of $57 per share, the highs in set in 2007 and 2006. There are numerous examples that correspond to this, including many banks such as Wells Fargo, and Citigroup.

Next, we are moving on to talk about specific industries in general and the unique risk that each one of them possesses.

First off is the infamous pharmaceutical sector, where millions of traders lose money each year, now before I go off on a rampage and make readers upset. This sector is very good for companies that already have a revenue base built up like Johnson and Johnson, but is horrible for companies who are in the PDUFA stage and who are trying to get their very first drug approved, because there are many examples where the trial has not worked out and shares go tumbling down, in these cases millions of shareholders lose the majority of their stake. As a side note many of these companies, are penny stocks meaning they offer a hefty reward but they also offer a hefty amount of risk. As an example and I would not refer to this as a penny stock, here is Intercept Pharmaceuticals which skyrocketed from a mere $60.28 per share on December 12th, 2013 to $460.21 on March 11th, 2014. These gains have brought investors huge gains of over 680 percent. But the problem is that these gains are very uncertain, the stock usually moves up approximately five percent on any given day which could also mean that the stock could plummet as much has gone up, this stock is very volatile and hence would not be a safe and steady long-term investment. Not saying it's a bad investment it just wouldn't be safe for your portfolio. But instead of investing in the trial phase of the respective company, what you could do is invest in the momentum, usually stocks build up in the months building up to the announcement of the company, stocks tend to move higher on sentiment and momentum. But emphasizing on the subject of this book don't get greedy sell even if a million signs point to the drug being approved sell, sell, sell.

Next is the technology sector, which is increasingly becoming known for its sentiment based trends. A very good example of this would be Facebook who unlike its peers worked hard at staying at its original IPO level of $38 per share, within a few months the stock hit lows near $20 per share, and shortly thereafter it moved up and down until one earnings report hit the market and shares have started to climb ever since. As shown sentiment was key in this as volume and shareholder expectation increased, the stock price started to drive up as well, proving that sentiment means everything.

With all of the above being said, you have to learn to be disciplined and sell at the right time, once you realize the goal you had originally set out for you should immediately sell because anything can happen.

Following the anything can happen guideline, always know not only the company's news but know and abide by the whole market's news. As in lets say Federal Reserve chairman Janet Yellen is speaking at a world conference or a new jobs report is due, do not and I repeat do not buy those stocks which are heavily reliant on news, this intern makes these stocks very volatile and would create a bad situation for you and your portfolio. At times following these events the markets end up 200 points in the red, imagine what this would do to stocks that rely on the overall market sentiment to go up and down for the most part.

Another growing concern these days, is the interference of hedge fund managers and celebrities interfering in the stock market, as an example lets say Person A is a hedge-fund manager lets say I am known as an investment icon in the financial world, I announce that I have initiated a 10 percent stake in stock XYZ, I bought the shares at $65 per share and announced my position right after the closing bell, in most cases the stock immediately skyrockets, this is obviously good, and in most cases the stock continues to spike higher due to investor sentiment, but now here is where greed comes into play, do not get greedy at this point the worst possible thing you could do for your portfolio is keep the stock. Instead

SELL IT! Selling allows you to recognize those profits on paper and build discipline, I can promise you the more you sell when you are willing to do so the more you gains you will realize in the long-term.

Before you go out and start trading you need to follow two very crucial steps; for the first month all you do is watch specific stocks, such as ABC, or XYZ continuously watch them and no other stocks, focus all your knowledge and scope on these stocks hopefully these stocks are less volatile and move but not as much as they should whether it be up or down. Once you finally believe in yourself then open a trading account, and start trading the stock in small quanities, always diversify, again doing so put a limit on your risk so if you lose some in one company it won't ruin your portfolio.

As mentioned above many times Greed starts out by being a hobby, you invest some money here and there in the stock market and other ventures that we will talk about later on, but then this eventually transitions to the later stages such as being a passion and eventually becoming an addiction. If you have the necessary know how you can prevent this passion of greed from occurring, and if prevented long enough this can lead to your success.

Again greed is an emotion, and emotions can be controlled. As a recap, for this section:

- First off try to not trade stocks at all
- Never invest in earnings
- Never hold a position over night
- Never buy a pharmaceutical based on Drug approvals or trials
- Hedge-Fund managers control the majority of the market if they buy into a stock
- And finally never give money to family for investment purposes

Real Estate

Real Estate is very tricky; you have to completely understand what you are doing even if it represents a small percent of your portfolio. Before actually purchasing a property, do not just look at the infamous Zillow Zestimate as it has proven to be often times wrong. Look up the tax values then the average number of houses sold in that respective area within the last couple of months, then look at the price per square foot trending within the past month, and then finally look at the report that comes with the real estate online. Your realtor should know what this is, many people often miss this and it costs then thousands of dollars later.

Fixer upper homes are usually the worst to buy even if they are very cheap, the majority of the time fixer upper's are only for people who are willing to and know how to do the necessary work requires. Do not get greedy and think it will be the world's easiest job, investment homes are usually the same deal

As tempting as it may be do not put a hefty down payment unless you need to or unless you have no other debt. This includes housing and credit card debt. Many and arguably so say that middle class Americans get rich by saving their money and paying rebutting off, this is partly true as you pay everything off your disposable income might increase yet you can only do so much investment wise with a 2000 in extra disposable income, instead focus on your daily job rather than cutting expenses, of course this is subject to a bunch if debate and is very controversial.

As many of my fellow financiers believe debt consolidation is key, when it come to paying debt off. You may be thinking, how does greed relate to any of this. I have known numerous example were people have lost everything they have in a matter if days they have pulled money from their credit cards and have invested it all whether it be in a local real estate property or the deadly stock market these are two of the biggest no no's as this can alter your or your family's well being.

Greed comes into play when you begin to either excessively purchase real estate beyond your means or when you refuse to sell. A man once said, "no one wants to sell when they are making money but want to sell when they are not making money" this very true as many people's net worth is in their home itself. In fact the majority of Americans do not do anything besides their daily job. Excessively buying can also function as an addiction because the more you buy, if things do not go the way you want them to, losses will skyrocket, and eventually you will hit the point of no return, where debt is far greater than owners equity. This theory is also inline with over expansion, expanding is always good as it means you have the financial ability to continue to grow your business, but when you buy too much at once, that's when we have a problem. At that point two major things can happen; one being you starts to lose focus on your business and everything starts to fall because management is too little and you are the only one running the company. The second point, and this is where things start to get ugly, is where your debt increases, whilst sales fall, this in tern can create a huge mess and can even ultimately prohibit you from ever expanding again.

Don't get me wrong but wouldn't you rather invest in a fairly large strip center or a business rather than a small condominium or residential property? In the beginning like all financiers; invest, invest, invest in small properties learn the basics, but then start transition to bigger and better properties. And above all remember to sell, then buy and then sell again. Remember this cycle as it is a cycle to success. Just look at the top 1 percent, all they do is sell, they sell millions of shares of their company to guarantee their profits, otherwise stocks fluctuate so much they might even lose half their net worth in a year. It has happened before to many smart individuals. This is why when you sell you retain if not all of the potential profits the majority of them, when you sell the business, property, or entity are profiting fairly well. If you remember this it can be very helpful, but if you forget it can haunt you forever.

As a recap for this section:

- Buy a small residential to start off with
- Transition to commercial complexes
- Never over expand

Algebra Time:

Table of Contents

Chapter 1: Order of Operations..3

    1.1: Identity Property of Addition...3

    1.2: Additive Inverse Property..3

    1.3: Definition of Subtraction...3

    1.4: Rules for multiplying Two Signed Numbers..3

    1.5: Rules for Dividing two numbers 3

    1.6: Identity Property for Multiplication...3

    1.7: Multiplicative Inverse Property 3

    1.8: Properties of Zero..4

    1.9: Commutative Property of Addition 4

    1.10: Commutative Property of Multiplication..4

    1.11: Associative Property of Addition 4

    1.12: Associative Property of Multiplication 4

1.13: The Distributive Property of Multiplication over addition and Subtraction 4
    1.14: Properties of Equality 4
    1.15: PEMDAS 4
    1.16: Basic Algebra Equations 5
Chapter 2: Linear Equations 8
    2.1: Finding the slope of Linear Equations 9
        3.1: Transformations 10
    3.2: Find the slope in standard form 11
    3.3: Substitution and Elimination 12
Chapter 4: Correlation and Scatterplots 19
    4.1: Scatterplots 19
    4.2: Line of best Fit 24
Chapter 5: Combining Like terms 26
    5.1: Combining Like Terms 27
Chapter 6: Rate of change/proportions 29
    6.1: Direct variation 29
Chapter 7: Probability 31
    7.1: Mean, Median, Mode 31
Chapter 8: Proportions/ratios 34
    8.1: Proportions 34
    8.2: Ratios 34
        8.3: Percentage: 35
Chapter 9: Exponential Functions 36
    9.1: Exponential Word Problems 36
Chapter 10: Inequalities: 40
    10.1: Inequalities 40
Chapter 11: Radicals 44
    11.1: Simplify Radicals 44
Chapter 12: Quadratics 46
    12.1: Factoring (Quadratics and by grouping) 46
    12.2: Expand: 51
Chapter 13: Shape Problems 58

13.1: Area Problems	58
Chapter 14: Absolute Value	62
14.1: Absolute Value	62
Solutions	64
Linear Equations	65
System of Equations	67
Correlation and scatter plots	68
Rate of change/proportions	69
Probability	70
Percentage	74
Exponential Equations	74
Inequalities	76
Radicals	78
Expand	81
Area Problems	84
Absolute Value	86

(I got the chapter 1 definitions from Holt Rineheart and Winston Algebra 1 Textbook.)

Chapter 1: Order of Operations

Linear equations can be complicated when it comes to addition, subtraction, multiplication in the same equation. There is an order in which these complicated equations needs to be solved. This chapter explains how to use basic rules to solve such types of equations.

1.1: Identity Property of Addition
For all real numbers b, 0+b = b=b+0 = b
ex1. 0+3 = 3=3+0=3

1.2: Additive Inverse Property
For each real number there is only one number so that b + (-b) = 0= –b + b = 0
2+(-2) = 0 =(-2) + 2=0

1.3: Definition of Subtraction
For all real numbers b-c = b+(-c)
3-2=3+(-2)

1.4: Rules for multiplying Two Signed Numbers

With like Signs you take the absolute value of each number and then multiply the two numbers together. With different signs (+) x (-) = - and (-) x (+) = (-)
3x(-1) =-3 and (-5) x 4 = -20

1.5: Rules for Dividing two numbers

(+)÷(-) = (-); (-)÷(+)=-
4/-2 = -2;-9/3 =-3

1.6: Identity Property for Multiplication

For all real numbers a x 1 = 1 x a = a.
5x1 = 1x5 = 5

1.7: Multiplicative Inverse Property

a is a real number. If a>0 then a x1/a =1/a x a =1
5x1/5=1=1/5 x 5

1.8: Properties of Zero

0 times any real number is zero.
0 x 5 = 0
0 divided by any real number is 0.
0/7 = 0
Any real number divided by zero is undefined.
5/0 = undefined

1.9: Commutative Property of Addition

B and C are real numbers. b + c = c + b
2+3 = 3+2

1.10: Commutative Property of Multiplication

b and c are real numbers. bxc = cxb
2x3=3x2 = 6

1.11: Associative Property of Addition

d,e,f are real numbers. d +(e+f) = (d+e) + f
1+(2+3) = (1+2) + 3 = 6

1.12: Associative Property of Multiplication

D,E,F are real numbers. d x (exf) =
(dxe)xf
1 x (2x3) = (1x2)x3 = 6

1.13: The Distributive Property of Multiplication over addition and Subtraction

1.14: Properties of Equality

$d(e+f) = de + df = (e+F)d = ed + fd$
$1(2+3) = 1(2) + 1(3) = (2+3)1 = 2(1)+3(1)$
$d(e-f) = de - df$ and $(e-f)d = ed - fd$
$1(4-3) = 4(1) - 1(3)$ and $(4-3)1 = 4(1) - 3(1)$

1.15: PEMDAS

The following rules are followed in order of operation also called as PEMDAS
Parenthesis, Exponents, Multiplication, Division, Addition, Subtraction
When reading an equation from left to right the acronym PEMDAS will explain the order on how to solve an equation. Solving an equation must be done in the following order parenthesis, exponents, multiplication, division, addition, and subtraction. For example in the following equation $(4-2)^2 + 3 \times 4 - 2$. First you solve what is in the parenthesis which is $4-2 = 2$. Then you simplify the term with the exponent so you get $2^2=4$.
The equation should look like $4 + 3 \times 4 - 2$. Then multiple the terms which need to be multiplied, $4 \times 3 = 12$. Now the equation should look like $4 + 12 - 3$. Now simply add 4 to 12 to get 16. Then the equation should look like $16-2$. Finally subtract 2 from 16 to get 14.

1.16: Basic Algebra Equations

To solve basic equation you must be able to get all the numbers to one side and all the variables to one side. In order to move all the numbers to one side you must use the opposite operations to what is presented in the equation. For example if one side has a 3 and you want to move it to the other side, you must subtract 3 from both sides of the equation.

Basic Equations Worked out Examples

Example 1

$3x+1 = 2x-4$

Step 1: Subtract 2x from both sides.
$3x - 2x + 1 = 2x - 2x - 4$
Step 2: Simplify
$x+1 = -4$
Step 3: Subtract 1 from both sides
$x+1-1 = -4-1$
Step 4: Simplify
$x = -5$

Example 2

$3x + 5 = 5x + 3$

Step 1: subtract 3x from both sides
3x-3x+5=5x-3x+3
Step 2: Simplify
5=2x+3
Step 3: subtract 3 from both sides
5-3=2x+3-3
Step 4: Simplify
2=2x
Step5: divide by 2
2/2 = 2x/2
Step 6 Simplify:
1=x

Example 3
30-2x = 4-5x
Step 1: Add 2x to both sides
30-2x+2x=4-5x+2x
Step 2 Simplify
30=4-3x
Step 3: Subtract 4 from both sides
30-4=4-3x-4
Step 4: Simplify
26=-3x
Step 5: Divide by -3
26/-3=-3x/-3
Step 6: Simplify
-26/3 = x

Problems

1. 3x+3 = 4x-2
2. 4x+3 = 2x-1
3. 3x+ 5 = 6x-7
4. 8x+ 4 = 5x-3
5. 3x + 5 = 4x-7
6. 9x + 5 = 4x – 1
7. 3x + 5 = 7x – 5
8. 7x – 5 = 8x + 5
9. 6x + 4 = 7x -7
10. 4x + 5 = 5x-1
11. 7x + 4 = 8x -5
12. 5x + 1 = 3x+4

13. $7x - 7 = 4x - 5$
14. $6x + 5 = 4x + 10$
15. $10x + 4 = 3x - 1$
16. $4x - 7 = 5x + 4$
17. $3x + 5 = 5x + 3$
18. $4x + 9 = 4x - 5$
19. $36 - 4x = 8 - 6x$
20. $x + 20 = 5 - 2x$
21. $7x + 12 = 5x + 3$
22. $6x - 7 = 9x + 4$
23. $5x + 10 = 3x - 7$
24. $8x + 5 = 3x - 9$
25. $3x + 10 = 5x - 9$
26. $3x - 7 = 4x + 7$
27. $10x + 10 = 9x + 8$
28. $3x + 4 = 10x - 7$
29. $2x - 5 = 5 - x$
30. $5x + 5 = 5x + 9$
31. $3x - 8 = 5x + 4$
32. $4x - 9 = 3 - 2x$
33. $3x + 5 = 7x - 4$
34. $x + 5 = 6x - 4$
35. $3x + 5 = 6x - 9$
36. $7x + 8 = 4x + 5$
37. $4x + 9 = 3x + 4$
38. $4x + 7 = 3x - 2$
39. $7x + 5 = 3x - 7$
40. $5x + 8 = 3x + 5$
41. $4x - 8 = 5x + 4$
42. $5x - 8 = 7 - 2x$
43. $3x - 8 = 8x + 5$
44. $2x + 9 = 3x + 4$
45. $5x + 5 = 6x - 9$
46. $7x - 9 = 6x + 8$
47. $3x - 5 = 6x - 3$
48. $5x + 8 = 4x - 9$
49. $2x + 5 = 2x + 7$
50. $4x - 5 = 5x + 4$

Chapter 2: Linear Equations

Linear functions have certain characteristics which set them apart from other functions. For example linear functions are straight lines with varying degrees of steepness, otherwise known as slope. This chapter will discuss how to find the slope of linear equations in both standard and slope intercept form., while also showing how to solve equations which have more than one variable.

Worked out Examples

Example 1 $y=3x+4$
Step 1: Isolate y.
$y=3x+4$
Step 2: Find the coefficient of the x term.
$y=\underline{3}x+4$
Step 3: Write down the coefficient of the x term.
3

Example 2: $3y = 7x + 3$
Step 1: Isolate y by dividing both sides by 3 or in other words divide every term by 3.
$3y/3=7x/3+3/3$
Step 2: Simplify
$y = (7/3)x + 1$
Step 3: Find the coefficient of the x term.
$y=\underline{(7/3)}x + 1$
Step 4: Write down the coefficient of the x term
7/3

2.1: Finding the slope of Linear Equations.

Find the slope of the following equations.

51. $y = 3x + 4$
52. $y = 5x - 5$
53. $y = 7x + 3$
54. $y = 8x - 2$
55. $y = 5x - 4$
56. $y = 3x - 1$
57. $y = 2x + 2$
58. $y = 3x - 9$
59. $y = 3x + 1$
60. $y = 7x/3 - 6$
61. $y = 8x - 1$
62. $y = 4x/3 - 1$
63. $2y = 3x - 1$
64. $3y = 9x - 4$
65. $2y = 11x + 3$
66. $5y = 12x - 4$
67. $3y = 7x + 3$
68. $6y = 5 - 2x$
69. $4y = 3 - 5x$
70. $2y = 5 - 8x$
71. $7y = 10 - 2x$
72. $-4y = 3x + 4$
73. $-3y = 2x + 5$
74. $-5y = 3x + 5$
75. $-4y = 3 - 2x$
76. $-2y = 5 - 3x$
77. $-7y = 9 - 4x$
78. $-4y = 5x - 4$
79. $-7y = -9x - 8$
80. $-9y = 10x + 4$
81. $2y = 3x + 5$
82. $y = 3x + 3$
83. $3y = 5x + 5$
84. $y = 4x - 1$
85. $y = -6x/3 + 5$

86. 2y = 4x + 5
87. 4y = 6y – 4
88. 3y = 5x – 6
89. 4y = 5y – 6
90. -3y = 5x – 5
91. y = 5x – 7
92. 4y = 6x – 7
93. y = 6y -5
94. 4y = 5x – 7
95. 9y = 7x -4
96. -2y = 5-2x
97. 9y = 6x + 5
98. 8y = 9x – 5
99. 10y = 7x – 5
100.   4y = 3x – 7
101.   2y = -7x + 5

3.1: Transformations

F(x) = x

To shift the linear function y=x in the vertical direction one must add or subtract numbers from the x in the original function. For example to move the function y=x vertically 2 units up the equation would look like this y=x+2. To move the function y=x down 2 units the equation would like this y=x-2.

To vertically stretch the function y=x, one must multiply the x in the original function. For example to stretch the function y=x by a factor of 3 the equation would look like this y=3x. To stretch the function by a factor of 1/3 the equation would look like this y=(1/3)x

y = x is the original function. Find the function after transformations have been applied to the original function.

102.   x+ 1
103.   x – 4
104.   3x
105.   2x + 4
106.   3x + 9
107.   4x – 1
108.   5x + 8
109.   -2x
110.   -3x + 5
111.   4x + 5

112. -3x − 5
113. -7x + 3
114. x + 3
115. 3x-5
116. -2x − 4

To find the slope of a linear equation in standard form one must use almost the same method as finding the slope in intercept form. The only difference is that the x and y terms are on the same side of the equation. The trick to finding out the slope of the equation is to get y by itself and then to see the coefficient of x.

Example 1: 8x+4y = 10

Step 1: subtract 8x from both sides
8x+4y-8x=10-8x
Step 2: Simplify
4y=10-8x
Step 3: Divide both sides by 4 or in other words divide each term by 4.
4y/4=10/4-(8/4)x
Step 4: Simplify
y=5/2-2x
Step 5: Find the coefficient of x.
y=5/2-2x
Step 6: Write down the coefficient of x
-2

3.2: Find the slope in standard form

117. 7x + 3y = 6
118. 3x + 2y = 5
119. 5x − 3y = 7
120. 2x + 5y = 8
121. 2x + 6y = 4
122. 10y − 6x = 5
123. 4x + 3y = 4
124. 2y − 8x = 5
125. 10y − 5x = 3
126. 7x − 8y = 7
127. 3x − 2y = 5
128. 7x − 3y = 5
129. 9x + 3y = 1

130. $7x - 3y = 9$
131. $5x - 6y = 3$
132. $3x + 2y = 7$
133. $8x - 2y = 5$
134. $9x - 2y = 10$
135. $10x - 3y = 2$
136. $9x - 3y = 9$
137. $3x - 2y = 5$
138. $4x - 5y = 9$
139. $3x - 5y = 5$
140. $7x - 5y = 4$
141. $9x - 6y = 15$
142. $8x - 7y = 8$
143. $7x + 3y = 10$
144. $3y - 9x = 4$
145. $2x + 3y = 8$
146. $2x - 5y = 8$
147. $9y - 2y = 7$
148. $5x - 3y = 10$
149. $7x + 5y = 3$
150. $4x + 8y = 9$
151. $9x + 5y = 10$

3.3: Substitution and Elimination: System of equations

There are two ways to solve system of equations. The methods are substitution and elimination. For substitution one must isolate a variable in one equation of the system of equations and then plug that in to the other equation. For example in the system of equations in the following problem, one can use substitution.

Example 1: $3x - y = -6$
$2x - y = -1$

Step 1: Isolate y in any of the equations. In this case the second equation $2x-y=-1$ will be used.

Step 2: Add one to both sides to $2x-y=-1$.
$2x+1-y=-1+1$
Step 3: Simplify
$2x-y+1=0$
Step 4: Add y to both sides
$2x-y+y+1 = 0+y$

Step 5: Simplify
2x+1=y
Step 6: Plug in 2x+1 to the y in the first equation which is 3x-y=-6.
3x-(2x+1) = -6
Step 7: Simplify
3x-2x-1=-6: Combine Like terms
x-1=-6: Add one to both sides
x=7
Step 8: Plug in x to any of the equations. In this case equation 2x-y=-1 will be used.
2(7) – y = -1
Step 9: Simplify
Multiply 7 and 2
14-y=-1:
Add one to both sides
15-y=0:
Add y to both sides
15=y:

Step 10: Write down the x and y values you found.
x=7 and y=15.

The elimination method involves adding or subtracting the two equations in the system of equations together in order to get one term to cancel out. This can be done in the following problem.

Example 2: $6x - 3y = 15$
$4x + 3y = 25$

Step 1: Find a variable that you want to cancel out by adding or subtracting. If you look closely at the problem you can see that you cant the x terms because no matter how you add or subtract 6x with 4x, you will never be able to cancel them out. But you can see that -3y and 3y can cancel each other out if you add them together. Thus the variable that you want to cancel out would be the y terms.

Step 2: Add or subtract the two equations to cancel out the variables.
$6x - 3y = 15$
+
$4x + 3y = 25$
_____
$10x + 0 = 40$

Step 3: Simplify
$10x = 40$
Divide by 10 on both sides.
x=4

Step 4: Once you found one variable all you have to do is plug it back in to any of the other equations to find another variable. In this case the second equation will be used.

$4(4) + 3y = 25$
Step 5: Simplify
$16 + 3y = 25$
Subtract both sides by 16
$3y = 9$
Divide both sides by 3.
y=3
Step 5: Write down the variable values
x=4 and y=3
Example 3:
$4x - 10y = 20$
$3x + 5y = 25$

If you understood the previous explanation of elimination you probably don't see any way for the variables to cancel out if you add or subtract them. So you probably want to use substitution. But there is still a way to use elimination. To use elimination you have to find a way to cancel out one of the variables. In algebra an equation is still the same if you do the same thing to both sides. So you can change 3x+5y = 25 to 6x + 10y =50. Those two equations are equivalent. If you look closely at the equation 6x + 10y =50, you can see that if you add it to the first equation 4x-10y =20, you can cancel out the y terms. So lets do that.

4x-10y = 20

+

6x+10y=50

10x+0=70
10x=70
x=7
Now plug back x=7 into any of the equations, in this case I will use the first equation 4x-10y.
$4(7) - 10y = 20$
Simplify
28-10y = 20
Subtract 20 from both sides
8-10y=0
Add 10y to both sides
8=10y
Divide both sides by 10.
8/10=y
Simplify
4/5=y.
Then finally write down the variable values that you found. x=7 and y=4/5.

Example 4

When you are solving a system of equations all you are doing is just finding where two linear equations meet. But sometimes you might find a system of equations which has no solutions or even infinite solutions. For a system of equations to have no solutions the two equations must be parallel to each other because if two lines are parallel it means they will never meet.
for example if you get a system of equations like in problem 167.
9x+2y=20
18x+4y=30

Example 5
The trick to finding out if two lines are parallel is to see if they have the same slope. So find the slope of both equations by using the methods described before. You should get the slope of the first equation to be -9/2 and the slope of the second equation to also be -9/2. So now that you know that same slopes means parallel and that parallel means no solutions. You should be able to deduce that the answer is no solutions. However you must be careful when doing this because sometimes even though two equations have two equal slopes, the answer might in fact be infinite solutions. Infinite Solutions is when the two lines are equal to each other. In this case the two lines have equal slopes but are not the same line thus the answer is no solutions. But in problem 174, the two equations are in fact the same line. Even though they may not look like they are equal to each other.
3x+5y=10
6x+10y=20.

If you multiply both sides of the first equation by 2 you should get 6x+5y = 20. That should look familiar because the second equation is in fact 6x+10y=20. Now that you have deduced that two equations are the same line in disguise, you can say confidently that the answer to this problem is infinite solutions. Think about it if two lines are the same line they are intersecting each other and infinite amount of times because linear equations never end in both directions.

Solve using Substitution and Elimination
    152.   5x-y = -7
                  x-y = -5

    153.   3x-4y = -16
                  x-y = -5

    154.   2x –y = -2

x-y = -4

155. 3x − 5y = 3
 8x − 10y = 7

156. 5x + 3y = 7
 5x + 8y = 9

157. 7x − 4y = 2
 6x − 8y = 7

158. 5x − 4y = 16
 3x + 4y = 32

159. 5x + 4y = 10
 10x + 8y = 14

160. 7x + 5y = 15
 14x + 10y = 20

161. 2x + 3y = 5
 4x + 6y = 7

162. X + 8y = 7
 3x+ 24y = 10

163. 9x + 2y = 20
 18x + 4y = 30

164. 5x + 6y = 20
 10x + 12y = 30

165. 7x + 8y = 17
 14x + 16y = 20

166. $4x + 3y = 7$
      $8x + 6y = 20$

167. $9x + 7y = 10$
      $18x + 14y = 15$

168. $7x + 8y = 4$
      $14x + 16y = 9$

169. $2x + 7y = 25$
      $4x + 14y = 30$

170. $3x + 5y = 10$
      $6x + 10y = 20$

171. $5x + 6y = 25$
      $10x + 12y = 50$

Chapter 4: Correlation and Scatterplots

The following chapter is about scatter plots and line of best fit. Scatter plots are mainly just data points which are plotted on graphs. To be able to decipher what these points are symbolizing, one must denote scatter plots into one of three categories. On the other hand lines of best fit are lines which will most accurately represent the data that is present in the scatterplots.

A positive correlation is when as when one variable increases so does the other variable. An example of a positive correlation would be in problem 177.

A negative correlation is when one variable increase, the other variable decreases. An example of a negative correlation would be in problem 82.

No correlation is when there is no relationship between the two variables. An example of no correlation would be problem 184.

Determine if the following is no correlation, positive correlation, or negative correlation

4.1: Scatterplots

172.

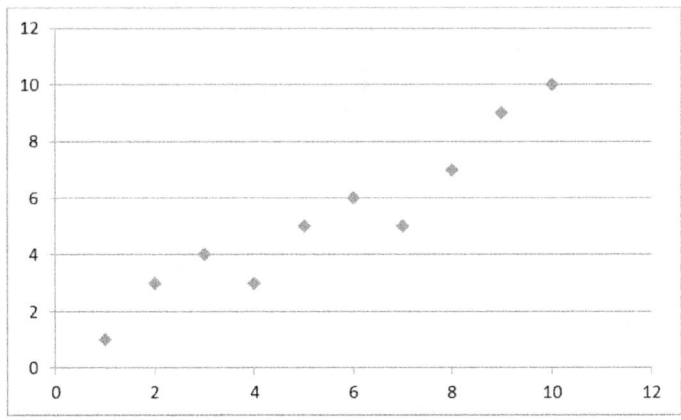

173.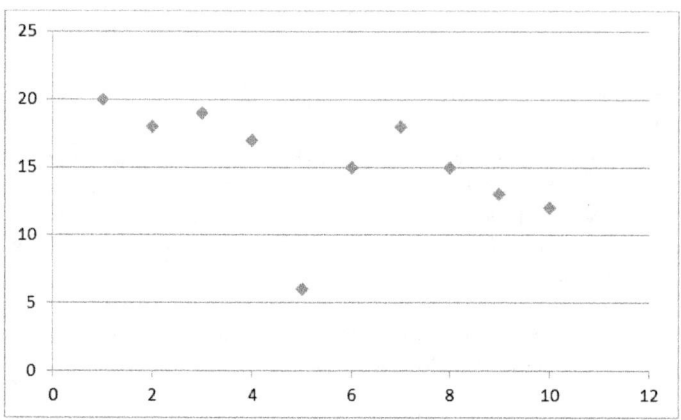

174.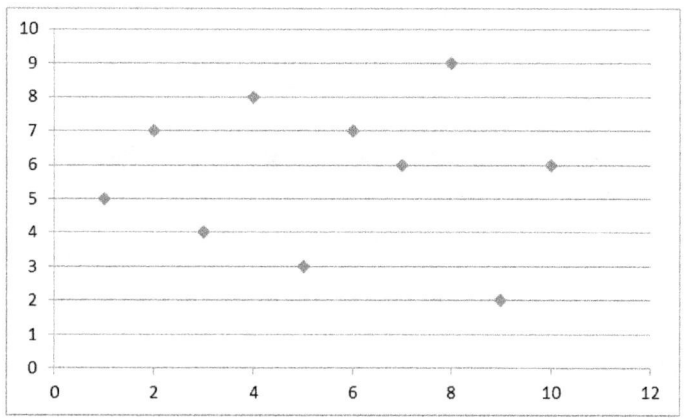

175.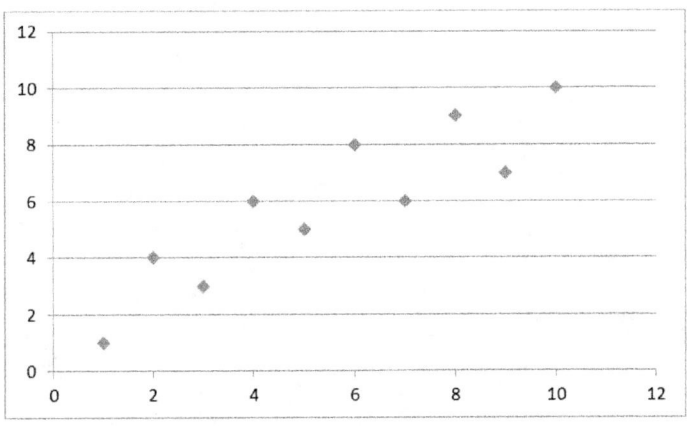

176.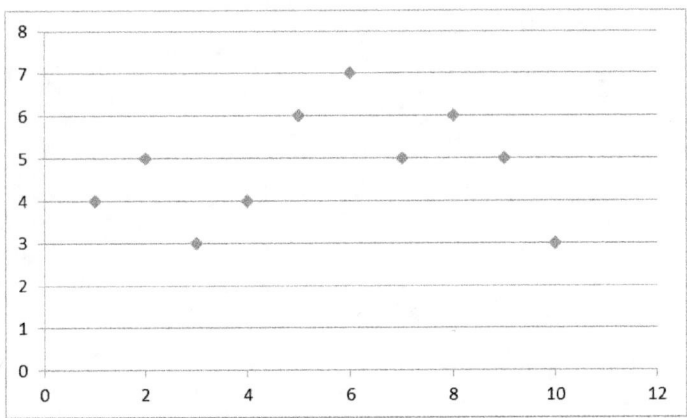

177.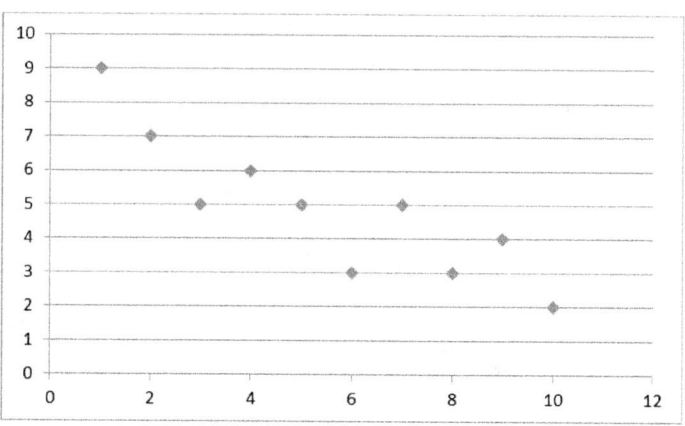

178.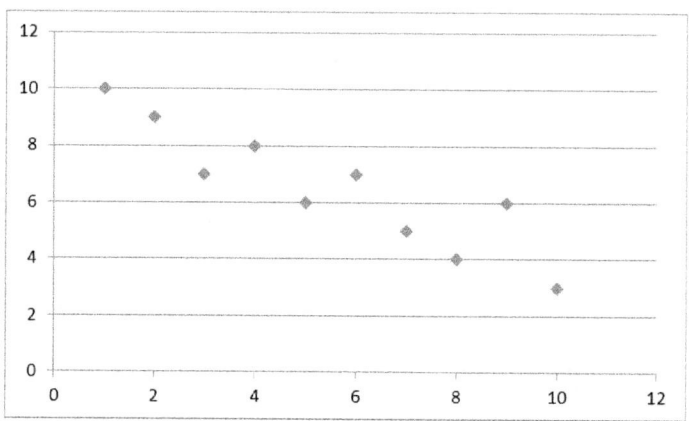

179.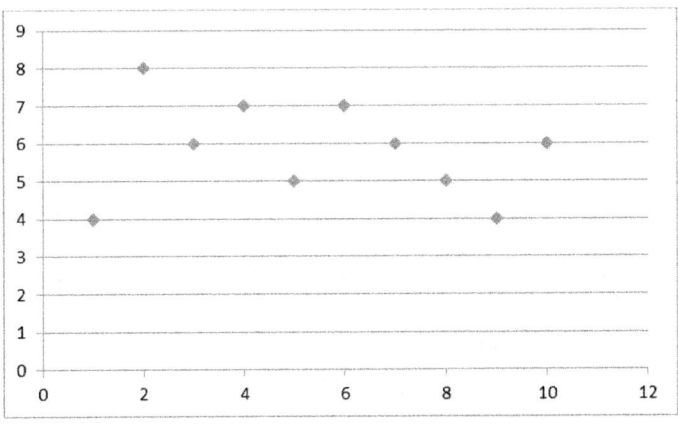

180.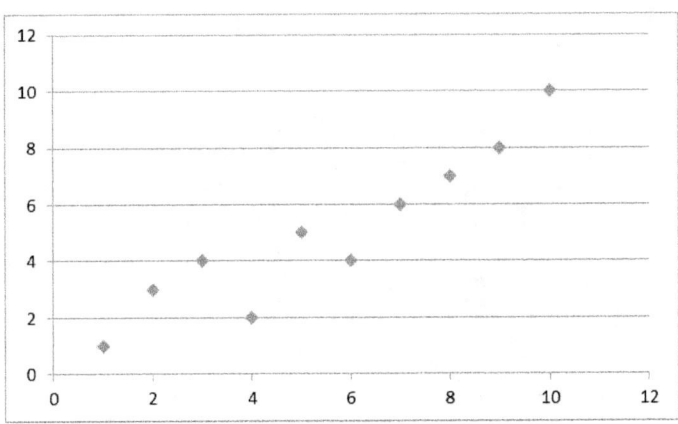

181.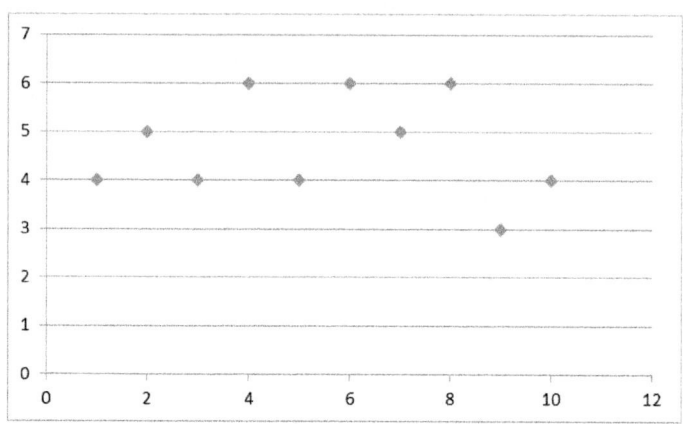

4.2: Line of best Fit

A line of best fit is a line which goes through as many data points as possible but also has the most equal number of points on each side of the line.

Which graph has a line that most accurately fits the data points?

182.
   Graph 1

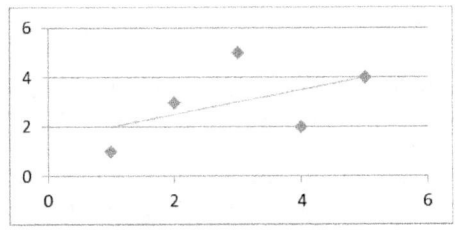

Graph 2

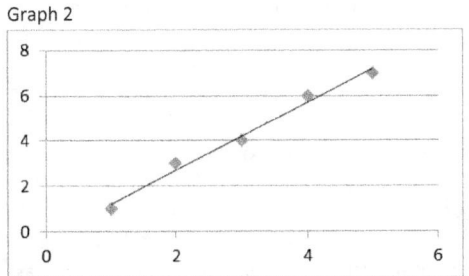

Which graph has a line that most accurately fits the data points?

183.
Graph 1

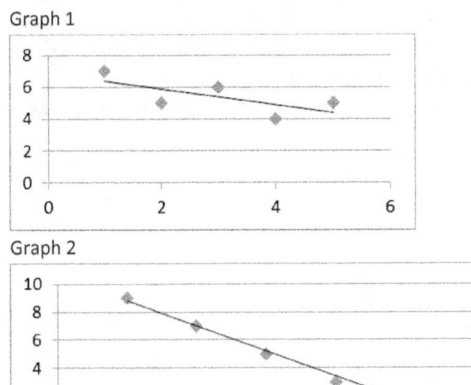

Graph 2

Chapter 5: Combining Like terms

Terms which can be combined should have the same variable with the same exponent on the variable. For example $3x^2$ and $4x^2$ can be combined since there are both x's for both terms and there is an exponent of 2 on the x of each term. However if the two terms were $4x^2$ and $3x$, they could not be combined since there is an x^2 in the first term and an x in the second term. Once you have deduced that the terms can be combined you must add up the coeffcients of the terms and keep the same variable and exponent. For example in the previous problem of $3x^2$ and $4x^2$, when you add these two terms together you should get $7x^2$. The 7 comes from adding 3 and 4 while the x^2 comes from the x^2 from each term.

Rules of exponents
When multiplying two terms with the same base, one must add the exponents of the bases. For example in the problem $y^2 \times y^3$ one must keep the same base but add the exponents of y^2 and y^3. Thus $y^2 \times y^3 = y^5$.
When dividing two terms with the same base, one must subtract the xponents of the bases. For example in the following problem y^4/y^2, one must keep the same base but subtract the exponents of y^4 and y^2. Thus $y^4/y^2 = y^2$.

Distribution of exponents
When there is a term or multiple terms are in parenthesis, and they are taken to a power there are certain rules which must be used. For example in the following problem of $(xy)^2$, the exponent must be distributed to each term. Thus the answer would be x^2y^2. This is the case when there is a coefficient within the parenthesis. For example for the problem $(2xy)^3$ you must distribute the exponent of 3 to the coefficient of 2 as well to x and y. Thus $(2xy)^3 = 2^3x^3y^3 = 8x^3y^3$.

5.1: Combining Like Terms

184. $(8x^2 + 7x - 3) - (3x^2 + 4)$
185. $3x^2 - 4x + 3x - 2x^2 + 7$
186. $5x^2 - 6x + 2x^2 + 3x + 6$
187. $6x^2 + 3x + 5 + 2x^2 + 6x$
188. $8x^2 + 7x + 10 + 3x^2$
189. $9x^2 + 5x + 7x^2 + 6x + 20$
190. $5x^2 + 7x + 5x + 19$
191. $(xy)^2$
192. $(4x^3)^3$
193. $(2xy)^5$
194. $(3x^2y^3)^3$
195. $(3x^2)(2x^4)$
196. $(4x^4y^2)^3$
197. $(6x^3(5y))^2$
198. $(5x^2y^4)^3$
199. $(6x^3y^3)^2$
200. $(2x^23y^3)^4$
201. $(3x^24y^2)^2$
202. $(2x^3)(3x^2)$
203. $(3y^2)(y^4)$
204. $4x^2/x$
205. $10x^3/5x^2$
206. $12x^3/6x^2$
207. $5x^2y^3/xy^2$
208. $7x^3y^4/7x^2y^3$
209. $5x^2 + 7x^2$
210. $3x - 4x$
211. $y^3 + 2y^3$
212. $8w - 9w$
213. w^3/w^{-4}
214. $6x^4 - (x^2)^2$
215. $3x^3 + 5x^3$
216. $y^4 - (y^2)^2 + y$
217. $(7x - 9) \times (7x-9)^{-1}$
218. x^3/x^{-2}
219. $5x + 10 + -5x + 20$
220. $4x^3 + 3x^3$
221. $2xy + 3xy$

222. $(3wxy)^2$
223. $2x + 3xy + 5yx$
224. $3x - 2x + 5$
225. $xy + xz + 3w + 2yx + zx$

Chapter 6: Rate of change/proportions

To solve a direct variation problem, one must first find the constant of variation or k. This can be done by dividing y by x. Once the constant of variation has been found, one can plug that constant of variation in to another equation to find an x or y value depending on the information given. For example if one knows the y value and the constant of variation, one can find the corresponding x value. Also if one knows the x value and the constant of variation, one can find the corresponding y value.

Example 1
For example in problem 230 you are given a y value and a corresponding x value with this information you can find the constant of variation. If y varies directly as x then the y and x relationship can be represented as y=kx. So now all you do is plug in the x value and its corresponding y value to find the value of k. 30=5k and now divide by 5 to find k. K equals 6. so now that you know k, you can use that information to find x in the problem. The other information that was given was that y=45. Then it asks you to find the corresponding x value. So since it is in the form y=kx and we know what k and y are we can find x. 45=6x, divide by 6 and then you find that x =45/6.

rate of change = change in y/change in x

6.1: Direct variation:

If y varies directly as x then y =kx or y/x = k where k is the constant of variation.
Y varies directly as x for the following equations.

226. If y=30 when x=5, find x when y=45
227. If y = 15 when x =3 find x when y=25
228. If y =25 when x=10, find x when y = 30
229. If y = 12, when x=4 find x when y = 30
230. If y = 20 when x = 2 find x when y=32.
231. If y = 18 when x=3 find x when y=24.
232. If y = 16 when x = 4 find x when y = 56.
233. If y = 12 when x = 8 find x when y=34.
234. If y = 17 when x = 5 find x when y = 10.
235. If y = 18 when x = 3 find x when y = 60
236. If y= 20 when x = 5 find x when y = 16
237. If y = 35 when x =7 find x when y=70.
238. If y = 27 when x = 9 find x when y=69
239. If y =28 when x =4 find x when y=77.
240. If y = 30 when x=6 find x when y=75.
241. If y = 65 when x = 4 find x when y = 76
242. If y = 50 when x = 5 find x when y = 85.

Find the constant of variation for the following problems if y varies directly as x.

243.   y=5 when x =2

244. y=3 when x=3
245. y = 5 when x = 3
246. y = 8 when x =2
247. y=9 when x=6
248. y = 5 when x = 4
249. y = 12 when x =6
250. y=16 when x =2
251. y=20 when x=4
252. y = 30 when x =5
253. y = 75 when x =3
254. y = 30 when x =6
255. y = 2 when x = 8
256. y = 2 when x = 6
257. y = 7 when x=4

Chapter 7: Probability

7.1: Mean, Median, Mode

The mean of the data.
To find the mean one must add up all the data in a set then divide by the number of data points.

Example 1
For example in the following problem (2,4,7,8,14), there are 5 points of data. Thus to find the mean one must add up all the data to get the sum which is 35. Then divide but the number of data points which is 5, thus the equation should be 35/5. The answer should be 7, thus the mean is 7.

The mode of the data.
To find the mode one must find the number which is repeated the most in a set.

Example 2
For example in the following problem,(1,1,2,2,2,2,3,4,5,7,7) the number 2 is repeated the most. Thus the mode in this example is 2.

Example 3
In the following problem find the mode (1,1,1,1,2,2,3,4,5,7,8)
The mode is 1 since 1 is repeated the most.

The median of the data.
To find the median one must find the number which is in the middle of a set when the set is listed from least to greatest or greatest to least.

Example4: In the following problem (5,3,4,2,1) if you line up the numbers from least to greatest, you get 1,2,3,4,5. Then one must cross out the numbers alternating from the numbers on the edge. For example first one would cross out 1, then 5, then 2 and then 4. The last number you are left with is 3, thus the median is 3.

Example 5: However if you have an even number of numbers in a set, then a different method is used. For example in the following data set(1,2,3,4,5,7) one must follow the same method in example 3 but at the end you are left with two numbers instead of 1. You are left with the numbers 3 and 4. To find the median one must take the average of the last two remaining numbers. Using the method from example 1 we find that the median is 3.5.

The range of the data.
To find the range of a set of data one must subtract the lowest value from the greatest value.

Example 6: For example in the following problem (1,4,6,9,10) subtract the lowest value 1 from the highest value 10 to get the range. Thus the range should be 9.
http://www.purplemath.com/modules/boxwhisk.htm

Box and Whisker Plot

To draw a box and whisker plot, one must find the median and the two sub medians. First start by finding the median of the data by using the aforementioned method in example 3, this will be known as Q2.Then after you find the median divide the data into sets. The first set is all the numbers left of the median(Q1) and the second set is all the numbers right of the median(Q3). Then find the median for the first set and the median for the second set. The medians of these sets are the sub medians.

Now create a number line and then make a box whose starting point is Q1 and whose ending point is Q3. Then within the box you created based off Q1 and Q3, draw a vertical line within the box in the corresponding Q2 value. Then to create the whiskers draw two lines, one line going from the box to the maximum value of the data and another going from the box to the minimum value of the data. Then draw a vertical line and the ends of each line to finish the box and whisker plot.

Example 7:

Plot a box and whisker plot for (1,3,5,7,9). First find the median of the data. The median of the data is 5(Q2). This was found by using the method in example 3. Then line up all the data left of the median to make set 1, (1,3). Then line up all the data right of the median to make set 2 , (7,9). Find the median of set 1. The median of set 1 is 2. Find the median of set 2(Q1). The median of set 2 is 8(Q3). Now create a number line and create a box using Q1 as the starting point and Q3 as the ending point. Then create a vertical line within the box at the corresponding value of Q2. Then create two lines. The first line should go from the box to the maximum value of the data, which in this case is 9. Then create another line which goes from the box to the minimum value of the data which in this case is 1. Finally create two vertical dashes at 9 and at 1.

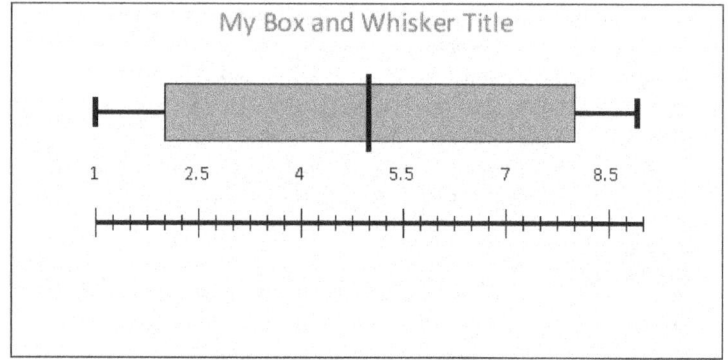

258. Find the mean of the number set (3,4,5,6,7)
259. Find the mean of the number set(1,3,5,7)
260. Find the mean of the number set (3,5,7,9,10)
261. Find the mean of the number set (2,5,7,8)
262. Find the mean of the number set(1,2,3)
263. Find the mode of the number set (2,2,2,3,4,4,5,5,6)
264. Find the mode of the number set (3,3,4,5,6,7)
265. Find the mode of the number set (4,4,4,5,5,7,7,8,8)
266. Find the mode of the number set (1,1,2,3,4)
267. Find the mode of the number set (5,5,7,8,9)
268. Find the median of the number set(1,2,3,4,5)
269. Find the median of the number set(2,3,4,5)
270. Find the median of the number set(1,4,6,8,9,10)
271. Find the median of the number set(4,3,5,7)
272. Find the median of the number set(3,2,5,4,7)
273. Find the range of the number set(1,3,5,6,7,9)
274. Find the range of the number set(1,2,4,7,8)
275. Find the range of the number set(3,5,7,8)
276. Find the range of the number set(1,2,4,7,8)
277. Find the range of the number set(3,5,9)
278. Find the range of the number set(3,2,4,5,9)
279. Find the range of the number set(4,3,10,6,4,8,5,4,5)
280. Plot a box and whisker plot for (2,4,5,7,8)
281. Plot a box and whisker plot for (2,4,6,8,10)
282. Plot a box and whisker plot for (3,5,7,9)
283. Plot a box and whisker plot for (1,2,4,7,9,10,11,12,14,15,17)
284. Plot a box and whisker plot for (1,3,4,5,7,8,11,14,15,16,17,18)

I got the chapter 8 problems ideas from this website
http://cdn.kutasoftware.com/Worksheets/Alg1/Percent%20Problems.pdf
I used different numbers than this website but the same kind of problems; I just want to make sure I don't plagiarize.

Chapter 8: Proportions/ratios

This chapter will discuss proportions, percentages and ratios.

8.1: Proportions

To solve a proportion one must multiply the numerator of the fraction of the left side of the equation with the denominator of the fraction on the right side of the equation and set that equal to the denominator of the fraction of the left side of the equation with the numerator of the right side of the equation.

Example 1: For example in the following problem the proportion is ½=3/x so we use the method aforementioned and we get 3 times 2 = x times 1. Thus 6 = x.

Solve.
285. 1/4 = 2/x
286. 2/5 = 5/x
287. 7/3=x/2
288. 5/4=y/3
289. 4/7 = x/3
290. 3/8 = y/3
291. 4/y = 5/9
292. 8/9=x/4
293. 4/7=5/x
294. 5/y=9/7
295. 3/8=y/5
296. 4/x = 7/2
297. y/8=10/3
298. 3/8=2/x
299. 7/9=y/4
300. 9/4=7/y

http://www.idiotsguides.com/static/quickguides/math/algebra-101-solving-ratio-word-problems.html

8.2: Ratios

To solve a ratio one must first get both sides of the ratio in terms of the same units. After this is done then one must simplify both sides by dividing by a common factor.

Example 1: For example in the following problem. What is the ratio of 4 inches to 4 feet?

Write the problem as a ratio 4 inches: 4feet. Then convert both sides to the same units. In this case the right side (4 feet) will be converted to inches thus the ratio is now 4 inches: 48 inches.

Now simplify the ratio by dividing by a common factor which in this case is 4. The ratio should now be 1:12.

Solve.

301. What is the ratio of 2 inches to 3 feet?
302. What is the ratio of 5 minutes to 4 seconds?
303. If a bag contains a ratio of 3:7 of green apples to red apples and there are 20 green apples how many red apples are there?
304. What is the ratio of 5 centimeters to 3 meters?
305. What is the ratio of 3 feet to 5 yards?
306. What is the ratio of 6 seconds to 7 minutes?
307. What is the ratio of 3 yards to 8 feet?
308. What is the ratio of 5 inches to 4 feet?
309. What is the ratio of 8 seconds to 5 minutes?
310. What is the ratio of 2 pints to 10 cups?
311. What is the ratio of 2 quarts to 5 pints?
312. What is the ratio of 4 pints to 7 cups?
313. What is the ratio of 100 ml to 1 liter?
314. What is the ratio of 3 liters to 1500 ml?
315. What is the ratio 5 liter to 200 ml?
316. What is the ratio of 3 liters to 100ml?
317. What is the ratio of 10 liters to 500 ml?
318. What is the ratio of 20 liters to 1000ml?
319. What is the ratio of 50 ml to 2 liters

8.3: Percentage:

A percent is the amount for every 100.

Example 1: Solve the following problem. What percent of 25 is 5? Write the problem into a proportion such as x/100=5/25. You should get x as 20. Thus the answer to the question is 20% or in decimal form .2.

Solve

320. What percent of 30 is 5.
321. What percent of 28 is 7.
322. What percent of 40 is 8.
323. What percent of 30 is 3?
324. What percent of 15 is 3?
325. What is 5% of 20?
326. What is 10% of 35?
327. What is 3% of 50?
328. What is 4% of 20?
329. What is 7% of 30?

Chapter 9: Exponential Functions

9.1: Exponential Word Problems

The trick to solving exponential equations is that one must transform the information from the problem to an equation. An exponential equation is of the following form $P=a(b)^x$. a represents the starting value, b represents the yearly change, while p represents the value after x years.

Example 1: Ocean Blue is a habitat which contains a population of sharks. The shark population doubles every third year and at year 0 the population is 90.

A. Write an equation which represents the exponential growth of the population.
   To find an equation one must know the starting value, the growth of the population, and how often the population is growing. The starting value in this case is 90, the growth of the population is that doubles, and how often the population grows is every third year. Thus a =90, b = 2 and the exponent is x/3. Thus the equation is $P = 90(2)^{x/3}$.
B. Put into words what your variables represent. a is the starting population at year 0. b is the growth rate of the population. x represents the years.
C. Use a graphing calculator to graph the equation you found.
D. Find out what the population is at year 6. Plug in 6 to the equation. $P = 90(2)^{6/3} = 90(2)^2 = 90(4) = 360$.
E. Find out what the population is at year 9. $P = 90(2)^{9/3} = P = 90(2)^3 = 90(8) = 720$
F. Explain why the y values of the graph can never be 0. The population was never below 0 or 0 and the population is growing thus the population can never be 0.
G. If the habitat can only hold 368640 members of the population, at what year will it reach its maximum holding capacity? Use a graphing calculator to find your answer.

In y_1 in the calculator put the equation you found in part A which is $90(2)^{x/3}$. Then in y_2 put the number 368640. Then graph the equations. Click 2nd then scroll down and click on intersect. The x value should be 36. Thus in 36 years the population will reach 368640.

Solve.

Forest Antler contains a population of white spotted deer. The deer population doubles every year and at year 0 the deer population is 100.

330. Write an equation which represents the exponential growth of the deer in Forest Antler.

331. Put into words what your variables represent.

332. Use a graphing calculator to graph the equation you found in 309.
333. Find out what the deer population is at year 5.
334. Find out what the deer population is at year 7.
335. Explain why the y values of the graph can never be 0.
336. If Forest Antler can only hold 3276800 deer, at what year will the forest reach its maximum holding capacity? Use a graphing calculator to find your answer.

River Troy contains a population of carp. The carp population triples every year and at year 0 the carp population is 20.

337. Write an equation which represents the exponential growth of the carp in River Troy.

338. Put into words what your variables represent.
339. Use a graphing calculator to graph the equation you found.
340. Find out what the carp population is at year 5.
341. Find out what the carp population is at year 7.
342. Explain why the y values of the graph can never be 0.
343. If River Troy can only hold 131220 carp, at what year will the river reach its maximum holding capacity? Use a graphing calculator to find your answer.

Island Flora contains a population of trees. The tree population doubles every other year and at year 0 the population is 50.

344. Write an equation which represents the exponential growth of the deer in Forest Antler.

345. Put into words what your variables represent.
346. Use a graphing calculator to graph the equation you found.
347. Find out what the tree population is at year 5. Find out what the tree population is at year 7.
348. Explain why the y values of the graph can never be 0.
349. If Island Flora can only hold 51200 trees, at what year will the island reach its maximum holding capacity? Use a graphing calculator to find your answer.

Lake Inferior contains a population of turtles. The turtle population doubles every third year and at year 0 the population is 80.

350. Write an equation which represents the exponential growth of the turtles in Lake Inferior.

351. Put into words what your variables represent. (P = population and y = years)
352. Use a graphing calculator to graph the equation you found.
353. Find out what the population is at year 6.
354. Find out what the population is at year 9.
355. Explain why the y values of the graph can never be 0.
356. If Lake Inferior can only hold 163840 members of the population, at what year will it reach its maximum holding capacity? Use a graphing calculator to find your answer.

Planet Purple contains a population of aliens. The alien population triples every other year and at year 0 the population is 120.

357. Write an equation which represents the exponential growth of the population.

358. Put into words what your variables represent.
359. Use a graphing calculator to graph the equation you found.
360. Find out what the population is at year 6.
361. Find out what the population is at year 8.
362. Explain why the y values of the graph can never be 0.
363. If the habitat can only hold 163840 members of the population, at what year will it reach its maximum holding capacity? Use a graphing calculator to find your answer.

Prairie Hooves is a habitat which contains a population of horses. The horse population triples every third year and at year 0 the population is 105.

364. Write an equation which represents the exponential growth of the population.

365. Put into words what your variables represent.
366. Use a graphing calculator to graph the equation you found.
367. Find out what the population is at year 6.
368. Find out what the population is at year 9.
369. Explain why the y values of the graph can never be 0.
370. If the habitat can only hold 6200145 members of the population, at what year will it reach its maximum holding capacity? Use a graphing calculator to find your answer.

Desert Heat is a habitat which contains a population of cacti. The cacti population doubles every year and at year 0 the population is 50.

371. Write an equation which represents the exponential growth of the population.

372. Put into words what your variables represent.)
373. Use a graphing calculator to graph the equation you found.
374. Find out what the population is at year 5.
375. Find out what the population is at year 7.
376. Explain why the y values of the graph can never be 0.
377. If the habitat can only hold 25600 members of the population, at what year will it reach its maximum holding capacity? Use a graphing calculator to find your answer.

Tundra Frostbite is a habitat which contains a population of penguins. The penguin population is cut in half every other year due to global warming and at year 0 the population is 1000.

378. Write an equation which represents the exponential decay of the population.

379. Put into words what your variables represent.
380. Use a graphing calculator to graph the equation you found.
381. Find out what the population is at year 5.
382. Find out what the population is at year 8.
383. Explain why the y values of the graph can never be 0.
384. At what year will the habitat have a population of 250? Use a graphing calculator to find your answer.

Jungle Primate is a habitat which contains a population of monkeys. The monkey population is cut in half every year and at year 0 the population is 500.

385. Write an equation which represents the exponential decay of the population.

386. Put into words what your variables represent.
387. Use a graphing calculator to graph the equation you found.
388. Find out what the population is at year 5.
389. Find out what the population is at year 8.
390. Explain why the y values of the graph can never be 0.
391. At what year will the habitat have a population of 125? Use a graphing calculator to find your answer.

Rainforest Rainbow is a habitat which contains a population of toucans. The toucan population is cut in a third every year and at year 0 the population is 900.

392. Write an equation which represents the exponential decay of the population.

393. Put into words what your variables represent.

394. Use a graphing calculator to graph the equation you found.
395. Find out what the population is at year 2.
396. Find out what the population is at year 3.
397. Explain why the y values of the graph can never be 0.
398. At what year will the habitat have a population of 1? Use a graphing calculator to find your answer.

Chapter 10: Inequalities:

Solving inequalities is very similar to solving basic algebra equations. The only difference is when you multiply or divide by a negative number the sign will be flipped. For example in the following inequality 5-2x>25
Step 1 subtract 5 from both sides
-2x+5-5 > 25-5
Step 2 simplify
-2x>20
Step 3 Divide by -2. Don't forget to switch the signs
-2x/-2< 20/-2
Step 4 Simplify
x<-10
Inequalities can be written in a form called interval notation. For example x>3 can be written as (3, ∞), notice how there are two parenthesis and that the left most number is the smallest the inequality can be while the right side is how large the inequality can be.

However if the inequality was x≥3 then you must use a bracket when writing the inequality in interval notation. Thus x≥3 can be written in interval notation as [3, ∞). Parenthesis are used when the interval notation doesn't include a number but the brackets are used when the interval notation does include a number.

10.1: Inequalities
Solve.

    $2x + 1 > 19$
399.   solve
400.   Write in interval notation

    $3x + 3 < 18$
401.   solve
402.   Write in interval notation

    $5x + 4 < 34$
403.   solve
404.   Write in interval notation

    $6x + 3 > 21$
405.   solve
406.   Write in interval notation

    $4x + 10 > 50$
407.   solve
408.   Write in interval notation

    $3x + 7 < 28$
409.   solve
410.   Write in interval notation

    $4x + 5 < 29$
411.   solve
412.   Write in interval notation

    $3x + 6 > 42$
413.   solve
414.   Write in interval notation

    $2x + 10 > 30$
415.   solve

416.   Write in interval notation

   4x + 5 < 21
417.   solve
418.   Write in interval notation

   8x + 12 < 36
419.   solve
420.   Write in interval notation

   4x - 1 > 15
421.   solve
422.   Write in interval notation

   3x – 2 < 16
423.   solve
424.   Write in interval notation

   5x – 4 > 36
425.   solve
426.   Write in interval notation

   6x – 7 < 35
427.   solve
428.   Write in interval notation

   7x -5 < 51
429.   solve
430.   Write in interval notation

   x – 8 < 19
431.   solve
432.   Write in interval notation

   x – 10 < 20
433.   solve
434.   Write in interval notation

   x – 7 > 34
435.   solve
436.   Write in interval notation

$2x - 3 > 25$
437.　　solve
438.　　Write in interval notation

$3x - 5 < 25$
439.　　solve
440.　　Write in interval notation

$4x - 2 > 14$
441.　　solve
442.　　Write in interval notation

$5x + 2 > 3x + 1$
443.　　solve
444.　　Write in interval notation

$7x + 3 < 2x + 4$
445.　　solve
446.　　Write in interval notation

$8x + 2 > 2x + 2$
447.　　solve
448.　　Write in interval notation

$4x - 3 > 3x + 5$
449.　　solve
450.　　Write in interval notation

$2x - 1 < 4x + 1$
451.　　solve
452.　　Write in interval notation

$3x + 1 > 2x - 2$
453.　　solve
454.　　Write in interval notation

$5x + 1 < 4x - 6$
455.　　solve
456.　　Write in interval notation

$2x + 1 < 2x + 1$
457.　　solve

458.   Write in interval notation

   $3x + 4 > 3x + 4$
459.   solve
460.   Write in interval notation

   $6x + 3 \leq 6x + 3$
461.   solve
462.   Write in interval notation

   $3x - 1 > 2x + 1$
463.   solve
464.   Write in interval notation

   $6x + 2 < 4x - 1$
465.   solve
466.   Write in interval notation

Chapter 11: Radicals
11.1: Simplify Radicals:
To simplify radicals one must break up the radical into 2 factors of the radical and one factor has to be a perfect square.

Example 1: For example in problem 440 the radical to be simplified is $\sqrt{48}$. Following the instructions you must then split $\sqrt{48}$ into two factors, one being a perfect square. A factor of 48 which is a perfect square is 16 thus we can rewrite $\sqrt{48}$ as $\sqrt{16} \times \sqrt{3}$. This can be further rewritten as $4\sqrt{3}$ since $\sqrt{16} = 4$.

Solve.

467. $\sqrt{48}$
468. $\sqrt{32}$
469. $\sqrt{98}$
470. $\sqrt{100}$
471. $\sqrt{108}$
472. $\sqrt{54}$
473. $\sqrt{40}$
474. $\sqrt{12}$
475. $\sqrt{200}$
476. $\sqrt{128}$
477. $\sqrt{80}$
478. $\sqrt{162}$
479. $\sqrt{150}$
480. $\sqrt{49}$
481. $\sqrt{81}$
482. $\sqrt{100}$
483. $\sqrt{121}$
484. $\sqrt{5} \times \sqrt{3}$
485. $4\sqrt{2} \times 3\sqrt{2}$
486. $\sqrt{24} \times \sqrt{72}$
487. $\sqrt{54} \times \sqrt{27}$
488. $2\sqrt{17} \times \sqrt{85}$
489. $7\sqrt{3} \times 5\sqrt{3}$
490. $3\sqrt{5} \times 6\sqrt{5}$
491. $2\sqrt{7} \times 3\sqrt{7}$
492. $3\sqrt{11} \times 5\sqrt{11}$
493. $2\sqrt{5} \times 4\sqrt{5}$
494. $4\sqrt{3} \times 5\sqrt{3}$

495. $7\sqrt{2} \times 9\sqrt{2}$
496. $3\sqrt{3} \times 7\sqrt{3}$
497. $2\sqrt{2} + 3\sqrt{2}$
498. $7\sqrt{3} + 5\sqrt{3}$
499. $3\sqrt{5} + 5\sqrt{5}$
500. $4\sqrt{7} + 3\sqrt{7}$
501. $6\sqrt{3} - 2\sqrt{3}$
502. $7\sqrt{6} - 3\sqrt{6}$
503. $3\sqrt{2} - 2\sqrt{2}$
504. $7\sqrt{3} - 5\sqrt{3}$
505. $3\sqrt{2} + 2\sqrt{2} - 4\sqrt{2}$
506. $4\sqrt{3} + 5\sqrt{3} - 4\sqrt{3}$
507. $9\sqrt{5} + 3\sqrt{5} - 6\sqrt{5}$
508. $10\sqrt{7} + 4\sqrt{7} - 2\sqrt{7} + 3\sqrt{7} - 6\sqrt{7}$
509. $\sqrt{108} + \sqrt{72} + 5\sqrt{6} - \sqrt{6} + 2\sqrt{6} - 3\sqrt{6}$

Chapter 12: Quadratics

12.1: Factoring (Quadratics and by grouping)

To expand two factors of a quadratic equation one must use the method FOIL. FOIL stands for first, outer, inner and last. In FOIL one first multiplies the first terms of the two factors, then the inner terms of the factors, then the outer terms of the factors, and finally the last terms of the factors.

Example 1: For example in the following problem $(3x+3)(2x+1)$ one must use foil. The first terms of the factors are $3x$ and $2x$ so first we multiple those and we get $6x^2$. Then we multiply the outer terms which are $3x$ and 1 together and we get $3x$. Then we multiply the inner terms together and we get $6x$. Finally we multiply the last terms 3 and 1 and we get 3. Now we add up all the numbers and terms together and we get $6x^2+3x+6x+3$. Then we simplify and we get $6x^2+9x+3$.

To factor a quadratic equation we must first understand the structure of a quadratic equation. Quadratic equations are in the form ax^2+bx+c. To factor a quadratic equation whose a value is 1 one must follow the following steps. The two constants of the factors will multiply to c and the two constants will add up to b.

Example 2: For example in the following equation $x^2+7x+10$ the factors will look something like this $(x+e\_)(x+f\_)$. The e and the f should add up to 7 and they should multiply to 10. To find two numbers which satisfy these conditions one must list out all the factors of 10, which are 1,2,5,10. Now you must pair these factors with each other so they equal 10, you should get 1 and 10, and 2 and 5. Thus two pairs in all. Now out of these two pairs which add up to 7. The answer is the 2 and 5 pair. So the 2 and the 5 are the e and the f. Thus you can write the factors as $(x+2)(x+5)$.

To a factor a quadratic equation when a>1 one must use factoring by grouping. Everything is the same as the aforementioned method but this time the constants in the factors should multiply to a number other than c.

Example 3: For example in the quadratic equation in the following problem, $4x^2 + 14x + 12$. The factors should add up to 14 but multiply to ac which in this case is 48. Using the aforementioned method we can deduce that the two factors which add up to 14 but multiply to 48 are 8 and 6. Then one must split the middle term in those two factors thus $4x^2 + 14x + 12 = 4\ 4x^2 + 8x + 6x + 12$. Then one can factor $(4x^2+8x)$ and $(6x+12)$. Then one can factor out $4x$ from $(4x^2+8x)$ and factor out 6 from $(6x+12)$. You should get $4x(x+2) + 6(x+2)$. Then one can factor out a common factor of $x+2$ from both terms and get $(x+2)(4x+6)$.

However sometimes a quadratic equation cannot be factored into integers, when this is the case one must use the quadratic formula. The quadratic formula can also be used when the factors are integers. The quadratic formula is $(x=-b\pm\sqrt{b^2-4ac})/2a$.

Example 4: For example for the following equation $2x^2-25+20$, the quadratic formula should be used. a=2, b=-25, and c=20. $x=25\pm\sqrt{(-25)^2-4(2)(20)}/2(2) = 25\pm(\sqrt{625-160})/4=(25\pm\sqrt{465})/4$. Thus the roots are $25+\sqrt{465}$ and $25-\sqrt{465}$. Thus the factors would be $(x-(25+\sqrt{465}))$ and $(x - (25-\sqrt{465}))$ or $(x-25-\sqrt{465})$ and $(x-25+\sqrt{465})$.

Solve.

$x^2 + 8x$
510.   Factor
511.   Solve

$x^2 - 6x + 9$
512.   Factor
513.   Solve

$x^2 + 11x + 30$
514.   Factor
515.   Solve   x=-5 and x=-6

$x^2 - 17x + 72$
516.   Factor
517.   Solve

$x^2 + 7x + 12$
518.   Factor
519.   Solve   x=-4 and x=-3

$x^2 - 3x + 2$
520.   Factor
521.   Solve   x =2 and x=1

$x^2 + 12x + 35$
522.   Factor
523.   Solve   x=-7 and x=-5

$x^2 - 10x + 24$
524.   Factor
525.   Solve

$x^2 + 7x + 10$

526.   Factor
527.   Solve

   $x^2 - 9x + 18$
528.   Factor
529.   Solve

   $x^2 + 13x + 36$
530.   Factor
531.   Solve

   $x^2 - 7x + 10$
532.   Factor
533.   Solve

   $x^2 + 10x + 21$
534.   Factor
535.   Solve
   $x^2 - 12x + 32$
536.   Factor (x-4)(x-8)
537.   Solve

   $x^2 + 12x + 27$
538.   Factor
539.   Solve

   $x^2 - 11x + 28$
540.   Factor Solve
   $x^2 + 14x + 40$
541.   Factor
542.   Solve

   $x^2 - 8x + 12$
543.   Factor
544.   Solve

   $x^2 + 4x + 3$
545.   Factor Solve

   $x^2 - 10x + 21$
546.   Factor Solve
   $x^2 + 15x + 44$

547.   Factor
548.   Solve

$x^2 - 15x + 54$
549.   Factor Solve

$x^2 + 14x + 24$
550.   Factor Solve
$x^2 - 15x + 36$
551.   Factor Solve

$x^2 + 10x + 9$
552.   Factor
553.   Solve
$x^2 - 14x + 33$
554.   Factor
555.   Solve
$x^2 + 10x + 25$
556.   Factor Solve

$x^2 - 15x + 26$
557.   Factor Solve
$x^2 + 17x + 42$
558.   Factor
559.   Solve

$x^2 - 17x + 70$
560.   factor solve

$x^2 + 21x + 54$
561.   factor (x+3)(x+18)
562.   solve x=-3 and x=-18

$x^2 - 20x + 64$
563.   factor (x-16)(x-4)
564.   solve x=16 and x=4

$x^2 + 16x + 60$
565.   factor (x+10)(x+6)
566.   solve x=-10 and x=-6

$x^2 - 18x + 77$

567.   factor (x-11)(x-7)
568.   solve x=11 and x=7

   $2x^2 + 44x + 242$
569.   factor
570.   solve

   $2x^2 - 6x - 20$
571.   factor
572.   solve

   $3x^2 + 22x + 24$
573.   factor
574.   solve

   $12x^2 - 22x - 14$
575.   factor
576.   solve

   $-2x^2 - x + 6$
577.   factor
578.   solve

   $9x^2 - 3x - 12$
579.   factor
580.   solve

   $4x^2 + 6x - 4$
581.   factor
582.   solve

   $5x^2 + 7x + 2$
583.   factor
584.   solve

   $3x^2 - 2x - 1$
585.   factor
586.   solve

   $3x^2 + 37x + 70$
587.   factor
588.   solve

$5x^2 + -11x - 12$
589. factor
590. solve

$14x^2 + 22x + 8$
591. factor
592. solve

$27x^2 + 75x + 28$
593. factor
594. solve

$16x^2 + 78x + 2$
595. factor
596. solve

$12x^2 - 13x - 14$
597. factor
598. solve

$16x^2 + 16x - 21$
599. factor
600. solve

$24x^2 - 42x - 27$
601. factor
602. solve

12.2: Expand: Solve using quadratic formula, and graph using graphing calculator.

$(3x+1)(2x+2)$
603. Expand
604. Solve using quadratic formula
605. Graph using graphing calculator

$(4x+4)(3x+2)$
606. Expand
607. Solve using quadratic formula
608. Graph using graphing calculator

$(3x+3)(2x+1)$

609. Expand
610. Solve using quadratic formula
611. Graph using graphing calculator

(5x+2)(4x-1)
612. Expand
613. Solve using quadratic formula
614. Graph using graphing calculator

(2x-3)(3x+4)
615. Expand
616. Solve using quadratic formula
617. Graph using graphing calculator

(3x+ 5) (2x+5)
618. Expand
619. Solve using quadratic formula
620. Graph using graphing calculator

(6x-1)(2x+2)
621. Expand
622. Solve using quadratic formula
623. Graph using graphing calculator

(4x-3)(3x+2)
624. Expand
625. Solve using quadratic formula
626. Graph using graphing calculator

(3x+3)(2x+5)
627. Expand
628. Solve using quadratic formula
629. Graph using graphing calculator

(4x-5)(3x-3)

630. Expand
631. Solve using quadratic formula
632. Graph using graphing calculator

(5x-3)(3x+2)
633. Expand
634. Solve using quadratic formula
635. Graph using graphing calculator

(3x + 7)(2x+8)
636. Expand
637. Solve using quadratic formula
638. Graph using graphing calculator

(3x-1)(2x+4)
639. Expand
640. Solve using quadratic formula
641. Graph using graphing calculator

(x+ 4)(x-5)
642. Expand
643. Solve using quadratic formula
644. Graph using graphing calculator

(x+3)(x+1)
645. Expand
646. Solve using quadratic formula
647. Graph using graphing calculator

(x+7)(x+8)
648. Expand
649. Solve using quadratic formula
650. Graph using graphing calculator

(2x+3)(x-5)

651. Expand
652. Solve using quadratic formula
653. Graph using graphing calculator

(3x+1)(x-4)
654. Expand
655. Solve using quadratic formula
656. Graph using graphing calculator

(2x+1)(3x-2)
657. Expand
658. Solve using quadratic formula
659. Graph using graphing calculator

(5x+4)(4x-1)
660. Expand
661. Solve using quadratic formula
662. Graph using graphing calculator

(3x+2)(x-1)
663. Expand
664. Solve using quadratic formula
665. Graph using graphing calculator

(2x+1)(x-10)
666. Expand
667. Solve using quadratic formula
668. Graph using graphing calculator

(3x+1)(2x+2)
669. Expand
670. Solve using quadratic formula
671. Graph using graphing calculator

(7x + 5)(6x+2)
672. Expand
673. Solve using quadratic formula

674. Graph using graphing calculator

(3x+4)(4x+8)
675. Expand
676. Solve using quadratic formula
677. Graph using graphing calculator

(5x+4)(3x+2)
678. Expand
679. Solve using quadratic formula
680. Graph using graphing calculator

(4x + 3)(6x+2)
681. Expand
682. Solve using quadratic formula
683. Graph using graphing calculator

(3x+9)(5x + 3)
684. Expand
685. Solve using quadratic formula
686. Graph using graphing calculator

(8x + 1)(7x-3)
687. Expand
688. Solve using quadratic formula
689. Graph using graphing calculator

(4x-2)(3x-4)
690. Expand
691. Solve using quadratic formula
692. Graph using graphing calculator

(2x+1)(x-1)
693. Expand
694. Solve using quadratic formula
695. Graph using graphing calculator

(9x+1)(x+3)
696. Expand
697. Solve using quadratic formula
698. Graph using graphing calculator

(3x-9)(2x+2)
699. Expand
700. Solve using quadratic formula
701. Graph using graphing calculator

(5x-5)(4x-3)
702. Expand
703. Solve using quadratic formula
704. Graph using graphing calculator

(4x+3)(4x+2)
705. Expand
706. Solve using quadratic formula
707. Graph using graphing calculator

(3x+5)(2x+7)
708. Expand
709. Solve using quadratic formula
710. Graph using graphing calculator

(6x-6)(3x-1)
711. Expand
712. Solve using quadratic formula
713. Graph using graphing calculator

(5x+9)(2x-7)
714. Expand
715. Solve using quadratic formula
716. Graph using graphing calculator

(8x+4)(5x+3)
717. Expand
718. Solve using quadratic formula
719. Graph using graphing calculator

(2x-5)(3x-6)
720. Expand
721. Solve using quadratic formula
722. Graph using graphing calculator

(4x+4)(7x-3)
723. Expand

724. Solve using quadratic formula
725. Graph using graphing calculator

(7x-6)(5x+8)
726. Expand
727. Solve using quadratic formula
728. Graph using graphing calculator

(2x+10)(3x+4)
729. Expand
730. Solve using quadratic formula (x = -10/2 and x=-4/3)
731. Graph using graphing calculator

(3x-9)(4x+2)
732. Expand
733. Solve using quadratic formula
734. Graph using graphing calculator

(4x-1)(x+1)
735. Expand
736. Solve using quadratic formula
737. Graph using graphing calculator

(5x-9)(3x+7)
738. Expand
739. Solve using quadratic formula
740. Graph using graphing calculator

(7x-7)(x+8)
741. Expand
742. Solve using quadratic formula
743. Graph using graphing calculator

Chapter 13: Shape Problems

13.1: Area Problems

This chapter will cover the basics in dealing with the area of circles, squares, rectangles, and triangles. This chapter will also review the Pythagorean Theorem. **Example 1:** If a circle has an area of 4 pi cm², what is the radius of the circle?

$\pi r^2 = 4\pi$
$r^2 = 16$
$r = 4$

Example 2: If a square has an area of 47cm² what is the side length of the square.

$x^2 = 47$
$x = \sqrt{47}$

Example 3: 1/2(base)10=100
base = 20

Example 4: If a rectangle is 10meters wide and its area 350 meters² what is the length of the rectangle?

base x height = area
10 x height = 350
height = 35

Example 5: A right triangle has a height of 3 and a base of 5, what is the length of the hypotenuse?

$3^2 + 5^2 = c^2$
$3^2 + 5^2 = c^2$
$9 + 25 = c^2$
$\sqrt{34} = c$

744.   If a circle has an area of 25pi cm, what is the radius of the circle?
745.   If a circle has an area of 36pi cm, what is the radius of the circle?
746.   If a circle has an area of 64pi cm, what is the radius of the circle?
747.   If a circle has an area of 121pi cm, what is the radius of the circle?
748.   If a circle has an area of 49pi cm, what is the radius of the circle?

749. If a circle has an area of 4pi cm, what is the radius of the circle?
750. If a circle has an area of 5pi cm, what is the radius of the circle?
751. If a circle has an area of 18pi cm, what is the radius of the circle?
752. If a circle has an area of 34pi cm, what is the radius of the circle?
753. If a circle has an area of 27pi cm, what is the radius of the circle?
754. If a circle has an area of 45pi cm, what is the radius of the circle?
755. If a circle has an area of 84pi cm, what is the radius of the circle?

756. If a square has an area of 50cm^2 what is the side length of the square.

757. If a square has an area of 34cm^2 what is the side length of the square.
758. If a square has an area of 84cm^2 what is the side length of the square.
759. If a square has an area of 92cm^2 what is the side length of the square.
760. If a square has an area of 29cm^2 what is the side length of the square.
761. If a square has an area of 10cm^2 what is the side length of the square.
762. If a square has an area of 72cm^2 what is the side length of the square.
763. If a square has an area of 92cm^2 what is the side length of the square.
764. If a square has an area of 36cm^2 what is the side length of the square.
765. If a square has an area of 31cm^2 what is the side length of the square.
766. If a square has an area of 97cm^2 what is the side length of the square.
767. If a square has an area of 70cm^2 what is the side length of the square.
768. If a square has an area of 73cm^2 what is the side length of the square.
769. If a square has an area of 29cm^2 what is the side length of the square.
770. If a square has an area of 94cm^2 what is the side length of the square.
771. If a square has an area of 82cm^2 what is the side length of the square.
772. If a square has an area of 84cm^2 what is the side length of the square.
773. If a square has an area of 90cm^2 what is the side length of the square.
774. If a square has an area of 15cm^2 what is the side length of the square.

775. If a triangle has an area of 100cm and has a height of 10. What is the length of the base of the triangle?
776. If a rectangle has an area of 50 cm^2 and a length of 10, what is the width of the rectangle?
777. If a circle has a circumference of 20pi what is the area of the circle?
778. If a triangle has a base of 10 and a height of 5, what is the area of the triangle?
779. If a square has a diagonal length of 10, what is the area of the square?
780. If a rectangle has a width of 20 cm and an area of 300cm, what is the length of the rectangle?
781. If the diameter of a circle is 20, what is the area of the circle?
782. If the diameter of a circle is 30, what is the area of the circle?
783. If the diameter of a circle is 50, what is the area of the circle?
784. If the diameter of a circle is 70, what is the area of the circle?

785. If the diameter of a circle is 52, what is the area of the circle?
786. If the diameter of a circle is 90, what is the area of the circle?
787. If the diameter of a circle is 20, what is the area of the circle?
788. If the diameter of a circle is 18, what is the area of the circle?
789. If the diameter of a circle is 28, what is the area of the circle?
790. If the diameter of a circle is 36, what is the area of the circle?
791. If the diameter of a circle is 34, what is the area of the circle?

792. If the radius of a circle is 5 meters, what is the area of the circle?

793. If the radius of a circle is 7 meters, what is the circumference of the circle?

794. A pool is thrice as long as it is wide. The pool is bordered by a fence which is 2 meters wide. The area between the pool and the fence is 60 meters squared. What is the area of the space inside the fence?

795. A rectangle is 7 cm longer than it is wide. If both dimensions are increased by 5, the area of the new rectangle will be 80 cm squared more than the area of the original rectangle. What are the dimensions of the original rectangle?

796. Rectangle A's width is half of its length. The area of rectangle A is 80 cm squared. Rectangle B's width is 5 more than rectangle A's width but Rectangle B's length is 7 meters less than Rectangle A's length. What are the dimensions of Rectangle B?

797. If a rectangle is 5 meters wide and its area 30 meters^2 what is the length of the rectangle?

798. If a rectangle is 6 meters wide and its area 54 meters^2 what is the length of the rectangle?

799. If a rectangle is 3 meters wide and its area 38 meters^2 what is the length of the rectangle?

800. If a rectangle is 9 meters wide and its area 83 meters^2 what is the length of the rectangle?

801. If a rectangle is 3meters wide and its area 94meters^2 what is the length of the rectangle?

802. If a rectangle is 8 meters wide and its area 32 meters^2 what is the length of the rectangle?

803. If a rectangle is 9 meters wide and its area 20 meters² what is the length of the rectangle?
804. If a rectangle is 12 meters wide and its area 74 meters² what is the length of the rectangle?
805. If a rectangle is 18 meters wide and its area 29 meters² what is the length of the rectangle?
806. If a rectangle is 16 meters wide and its area 30 meters² what is the length of the rectangle?
807. If a rectangle is 10 meters wide and its area 50 meters² what is the length of the rectangle?
808. If a rectangle is 7 meters wide and its area 56 meters² what is the length of the rectangle?
809. If a rectangle is 9 meters wide and its area 36 meters² what is the length of the rectangle?
810. If a rectangle is 12 meters wide and its area 60 meters² what is the length of the rectangle?

811. A right triangle has a height of 10 and a base of 5, what is the length of the hypotenuse?
812. A right triangle has a height of 4 and a base of 7, what is the length of the hypotenuse?
813. A right triangle has a height of 3 and a base of 9, what is the length of the hypotenuse?

814. A right triangle has a height of 3 and a base of 8, what is the length of the hypotenuse?
815. A right triangle has a height of 5 and a base of 5, what is the length of the hypotenuse?
816. A right triangle has a height of 3 and a base of 7, what is the length of the hypotenuse?
817. A right triangle has a height of 3 and a base of 4, what is the length of the hypotenuse?
818. A right triangle has a height of 6 and a base of 8, what is the length of the hypotenuse?
819. A right triangle has a height of 12 and a base of 5, what is the length of the hypotenuse?
820. A right triangle has a height of 4 and a base of 7, what is the length of the hypotenuse?

821. A right triangle has a height of 10 and a base of 9, what is the length of the hypotenuse?
822. A right triangle has a height of 11 and a base of 7, what is the length of the hypotenuse?
823. A right triangle has a height of 15 and a base of 25, what is the length of the hypotenuse?

824. A right triangle has a height of 3 and a base of 4, what is the length of the hypotenuse?
825. A right triangle has a hypotenuse of 10 and the height of the triangle is 6. What is the length of the base of the triangle?
826. A right triangle has a height of 7 and a base of 10 what is the length of the hypotenuse?

Chapter 14: Absolute Value

Find the absolute value of each of the following numbers

14.1: Absolute Value

To solve absolute value problems you must simply combine like terms within the absolute value signs then turn it positive. If the simplified number is already positive then just take out the absolute value sign.
Example 1: $|32| = 32$
Example 2: $|-27| = 27$

827. -45
828. 98
829. 24
830. -5
831. 92
832. 7
833. 9
834. -10

Find the absolute value of the following.
835. $|3-5|$
836. $|4-5|$

837. |3-7|
838. |6-3|
839. |7-5|
840. |9-4|
841. |5-8|
842. |3-10|
843. 92
844. 9
845. |5-8|
846. |3+5-7+9|
847. |5-3+9+4-20|
848. |6-5+4-7|
849. |5-4+7-9|
850. |5-7+9|
851. |5-9+3-10|
852. |3+ 5-7 + 8|
853. |3+5-9+8|
854. |3-9-6-5|
855. |4+5+9-30|
856. |2-9|
857. |5+(-3)|
858. |4+(-7)|
859. |5+(-9)|
860. |9+(-10)|
861. |4+(-7)|
862. |3+(-4)|
863. |4+(-8)|
864. |3+(-3)|
865. |5+(-8)|
866. |(-7)+8|
867. |4+(-4)|

Solutions

1. x=5
2. x= - 2
3. x=4
4. x=-7/3
5. x=12
6. x = -6/5
7. x = 5/2
8. x=-10
9. x=11
10. x=6
11. x=9
12. x=3/2
13. x=2/3
14. x=5/2
15. x=-5/7
16. x=-11
17. x=1
18. no solutions
19. x=-14
20. x=-5
21. x=-9/2
22. x=-11/3
23. x=-17/2
24. x=-14/5
25. x=19/2
26. x=-14
27. x=-2
28. x=11/7
29. x=10/3
30. no solutions
31. x=-6
32. x=2
33. x=9/4
34. x=9/5
35. x=14/3

36. x = -1
37. x=-5
38. x=-9
39. x=-3
40. x=-3/2
41. x=-12
42. x=15/7
43. x=-13/5
44. x=5
45. x=14
46. x=17
47. x=-2/3
48. x=-1
49. no solutions
50. x=-9

Linear Equations:
51. 3
52. 5
53. 7
54. 8
55. 5
56. 3
57. 2
58. 3
59. 3
60. 7/3
61. 8
62. 4/3
63. 3/2
64. 3
65. 11/2
66. 12/5
67. 7/3
68. -1/3
69. -5/4
70. -4
71. -2/7
72. -3/4
73. -2/3
74. -3/5
75. ½

76. 3/2
77. 4/7
78. -5/4
79. 9/7
80. -10/9
81. 3/2
82. 3
83. 5/3
84. 4
85. -2
86. 2
87. 3/2
88. 5/3
89. 5/4
90. -5/3
91. 5
92. 3/2
93. 6
94. 5/4
95. 7/9
96. 1
97. 2/3
98. 9/8
99. 7/10
100. ¾
101. -7/2
102. 1 up
103. 4 down
104. vertical stretch of 3
105. vertical stretch of 2 and 4 up
106. vertical stretch of 3 and 9 up
107. vertical stretch of 4 and 1 down
108. vertical stretch of 5 and 8 up
109. vertical stretch of 2 and goes in opposite in direction
110. vertical; stretch of 3, goes in opposite direction and vertical shift of 5
111. vertical stretch of 4 and vertical shift of 5
112. vertical stretch of 3, goes in opposite direction and vertical shift of -5
113. vertical stretch of 7, goes in opposite direction and vertical shift of 3
114. vertical shift of 3
115. vertical stretch of 3 and vertical shift of -5
116. vertical stretch of -2, goes in opposite direction and vertical shift of -4

117.	-7/3
118.	-2/3
119.	5/3
120.	-2/5
121.	-1/3
122.	3/5
123.	-4/3
124.	4
125.	½
126.	7/8
127.	3/2
128.	7/3
129.	x= -3
130.	7/3
131.	5/6
132.	-3/2
133.	4
134.	9/2
135.	10/3
136.	3
137.	3/2
138.	4/5
139.	5/3
140.	7/5
141.	3/2
142.	8/7
143.	-7/3
144.	3
145.	-2/3
146.	2/5
147.	9/2
148.	5/3
149.	-7/5
150.	-1/2
151.	-9/5

System of Equations

152.	(-1/2,-3/2)
153.	(-4,1)
154.	(2,6)

155.	(.5,-.3)	
156.	(1.16,.4)	
157.	(-.375, -1.15625)	
158.	(6,14/4)	
159.	no solutions (parallel)	
160.	no solutions	
161.	no solutions	
162.	no solutions	
163.	no solutions	
164.	no solutions	
165.	no solutions	
166.	parallel	
167.	parallel	
168.	parallel	
169.	parallel	
170.	infinite solutions	
171.	infinite solutions	

Correlation and scatter plots

172.	positive
173.	positive
174.	no correlation
175.	positive
176.	no correlation
177.	negative
178.	negative
179.	no correlation
180.	positive
181.	no correlation
182.	graph 2
183.	graph 2
184.	$(5x^2 + 7x - 7)$
185.	$(x^2 - x + 7)$
186.	$(3x^2 - 3x + 6)$
187.	$(8x^2+9x + 5)$
188.	$(11x^2+7x+10)$
189.	$(16x^2+ 11x +20)$
190.	$(5x^2+12x+19)$
191.	(x^2y^2)
192.	$(64x^9)$

193. $(32x^5)$
194. $(27x^6y^9)$
195. $(6x^6)$
196. $(64x^{12}y^6)$
197. $(900x^6y^2)$
198. $(125x^6y^{12})$
199. $(36x^6y^6)$
200. $(1296x^8y^{12})$
201. $(144x^4y^4)$
202. $(6x^5)$
203. $(3y^6)$
204. $(4x)$
205. $(2x)$
206. $(2x)$
207. $(5xy)$
208. (xy)
209. $7x^2$
210. $-x$
211. $3y^3$
212. $-w$
213. w^7
214. $5x^4$
215. $8x^3$
216. y
217. 1
218. x^5
219. 30
220. $7x^3$
221. $5xy$
222. $9w^2x^2y^2$
223. $7xy + 2x$
224. $x+5$
225. $3xy+2xz+3w$

Rate of change/proportions

226. $45/6$
227. 5
228. 12
229. 10
230. 3.2

231.	4
232.	14
233.	68/3
234.	50/17
235.	10
236.	4
237.	14
238.	23
239.	11
240.	15
241.	304/65
242.	8.5
243.	2.5
244.	1
245.	5/3
246.	4
247.	3/2
248.	5/4
249.	2
250.	8
251.	5
252.	6
253.	25
254.	5
255.	¼
256.	1/3
257.	7/4

Probability

258.	5
259.	4
260.	6.8
261.	5.5
262.	2
263.	2
264.	3
265.	4
266.	1
267.	5
268.	3

269. 3.5
270. 7
271. 4.5
272. 4
273. 8
274. 7
275. 1
276. 5
277. 6
278. 7
279. 7

280.
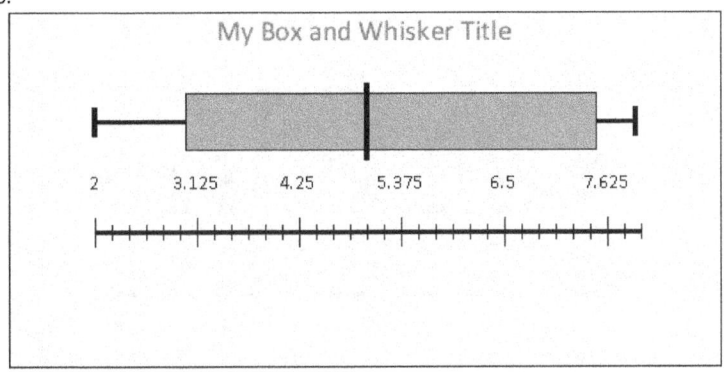

281.

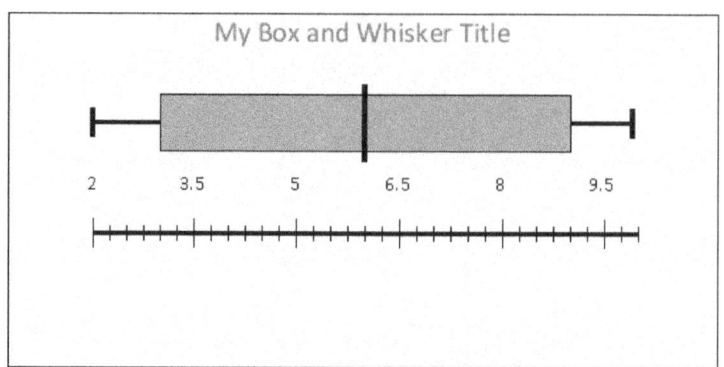

282.

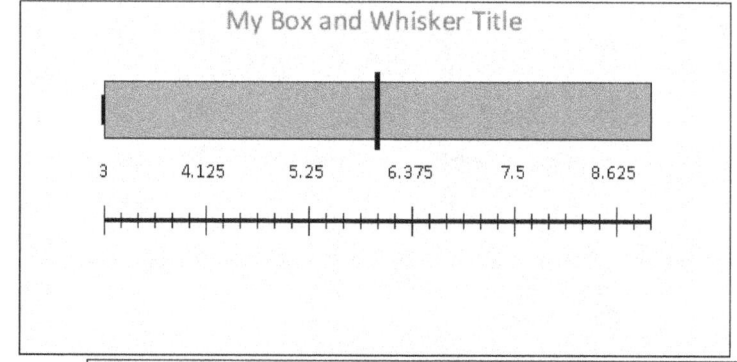

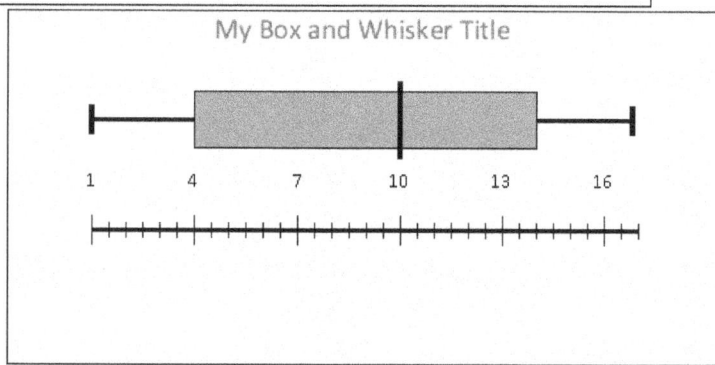

283.

284.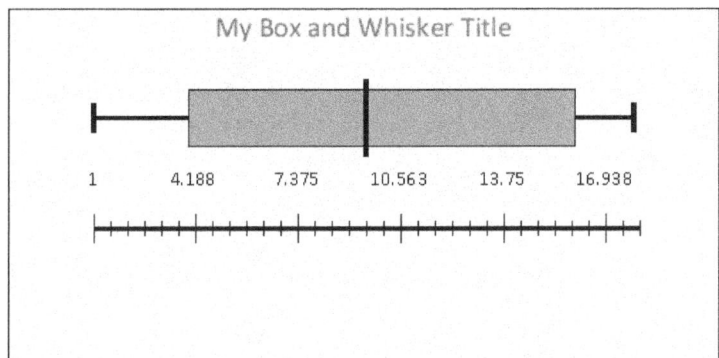

285. 8
286. 25/2
287. 14/3
288. 15/4
289. 12/7
290. 9/8
291. 36/5
292. 32/9
293. 35/4
294. 35/9
295. 15/8
296. 8/7
297. 80/3
298. 16/3
299. 28/9
300. 28/9
301. 1:18
302. 75:1
303. 140/3
304. 1:60
305. 1:5
306. 1:70
307. 3:1
308. 5:48
309. 2:75
310. 2:5
311. 4:5
312. 8:7

313.	4:5	
314.	1:10	
315.	2:1	
316.	25:1	
317.	30:1	
318.	1:20	
319.	1:40	

Percentage

320.	16.67%
321.	25%
322.	20%
323.	10%
324.	20%
325.	1
326.	3.5
327.	6
328.	.8
329.	2.1

Exponential Equations

330.	$P = (2^y)(100)$
331.	(P = population and y = years)
332.	Use a graphing calculator to graph the equation you found in 309.
333.	(3200)
334.	(12800)
335.	(exponential functions have a horizontal asymptote at y=0.)
336.	(year 15)
337.	$P = (3^y)(20)$
338.	(P = population and y = years)
339.	Use a graphing calculator to graph the equation you found.
340.	(4860)
341.	(12800)
342.	(exponential functions have a horizontal asymptote at y=0.)
343.	(year 8)
344.	$P = (2^{y/2})(50)$
345.	(P = population and y = years)
346.	Use a graphing calculator to graph the equation you found.
347.	(282)
348.	(565)

349. (exponential functions have a horizontal asymptote at y=0.)
350. (year 20)
351. $P = (2^{y/3})(80)$
352. Use a graphing calculator to graph the equation you found.
353. (320)
354. (640)
355. (exponential functions have a horizontal asymptote at y=0.)
356. (year 33)
357. $P = (3^{y/2})(120)$
358. (P = population and y = years)
359. Use a graphing calculator to graph the equation you found.
360. (3240)
361. (9720)
362. (exponential functions have a horizontal asymptote at y=0.)
363. (year 33)
364. (year 36)
365. $P = (3^{y/3})(105)$
366. (P = population and y = years)
367. (945)
368. (2835)
369. (exponential functions have a horizontal asymptote at y=0.)
370. (year 30)
371. $P = (2^y)(50)$
372. (P = population and y = years
373. Use a graphing calculator to graph the equation you found.
374. (1600)
375. (6400)
376. (exponential functions have a horizontal asymptote at y=0.)
377. (year 9)
378. $P = (.5^{y/2})(1000)$
379. (P = population and y = years)
380. Use a graphing calculator to graph the equation you found.
381. (176)
382. (62)
383. (exponential functions have a horizontal asymptote at y=0.)
384. (year 4)
385. $P=(.5^y)(500)$
386. (P = population and y = years)
387. Use a graphing calculator to graph the equation you found.
388. (15)
389. (1)
390. (exponential functions have a horizontal asymptote at y=0.)

391. (year 2)
392. P = (1/3)^y(900)
393. (P = population and y = years)
394. Use a graphing calculator to graph the equation you found.
395. (100)
396. (33)
397. (exponential functions have a horizontal asymptote at y=0.)
398. (year 4)

Inequalities

399. (x>9)
400. (9,∞)
401. (x<5)
402. (-∞,5)
403. (x<6)
404. (-∞,6)
405. (x> 3)
406. (3, ∞)
407. (x > 10)
408. (10, ∞)
409. (x < 7)
410. (-∞,7)
411. (x < 6)
412. (-∞,6)
413. (x > 12)
414. (12, ∞)
415. (x>10)
416. (10, ∞)
417. (x<4)
418. (-∞,4)
419. (x<3)
420. (-∞,3)
421. (x>6)
422. (6, ∞)
423. (x>4)
424. (4, ∞)
425. (x>8)
426. (8, ∞)
427. (x<7)

428.	(-∞,7)
429.	(x<8)
430.	(-∞,8)
431.	(x<27)
432.	(-∞,27)
433.	(x<30)
434.	(-∞,30)
435.	(x > 41)
436.	(41, ∞)
437.	(x > 14)
438.	(14, ∞)
439.	(x < 10)
440.	(-∞,10)
441.	(x>4)
442.	(4, ∞)
443.	(x>-1/2)
444.	(-1/2, ∞)
445.	(x<1/5)
446.	(-∞,1/5)
447.	(x > 0)
448.	(0, ∞)
449.	(x>8)
450.	(8, ∞)
451.	(x>-1)
452.	(-1, ∞)
453.	(x>-3)
454.	(-3, ∞)
455.	(x<-7)
456.	(-7, ∞)
457.	(no solutions)
458.	n/a
459.	(no solutions)
460.	n/a
461.	(infinite solutions)
462.	(-∞,∞)
463.	(x > 2)
464.	(2, ∞)
465.	(x<-3/2)
466.	(-∞,-3/2)

Radicals

467.	(4√3)

468. (4√2)
469. (7√2)
470. (10)
471. (6√3)
472. (3√6)
473. (2√10)
474. (2√3)
475. (10√2)
476. (8√2)
477. (4√5)
478. (9√2)
479. (5√6)
480. (7)
481. (9)
482. (10)
483. (11)
484. (√15)
485. (24)
486. (24√3)
487. (27√2)
488. (34√5)
489. (105)
490. (90)
491. (42)
492. (165)
493. (40)
494. (60)
495. (126)
496. (63)
497. (5√2)
498. (12√3)
499. (8√5)
500. (7√7)
501. (4√3)
502. (4√6)
503. (√2)
504. (2√3)
505. (√2)
506. (5√3)
507. (6√5)
508. (9√3)
509. (6√3 + 6√2 + 3√6)

Quadratics

510.	x(x+8)
511.	x=0 and x= -8
512.	$(x-3)^2$
513.	x=3
514.	(x+5)(x+6)
515.	x=5 and x=-6
516.	(x-9)(x-8)
517.	x = 9 and x=8
518.	(x+4)(x+3)
519.	x= -4 and x=-3
520.	(x-2)(x-1)
521.	x=2 and x=1
522.	(x+7)(x+5)
523.	x=-7 and x=-5
524.	(x-6)(x-4)
525.	x=6 and x=4
526.	(x+5)(x+2)
527.	x =-5 and x=-2
528.	(x-6)(x-3)
529.	x = 6 and x=3
530.	(x+9)(x+4)
531.	x=-9 and x=-4
532.	(x-5)(x-2)
533.	x=5 and x=2
534.	(x+7)(x+3)
535.	x=-7 and x=-3
536.	x= 4 and x=8
537.	(x+9)(x+3)
538.	x = -9 and x=-3
539.	(x-7)(x-4)
540.	x=7 and x=4
541.	(x+10)(x+4)
542.	x=-10 and x=-4
543.	(x-6)(x-2)
544.	x=6 and x=2
545.	(x+3)(x+1)
546.	x=-3 and x=-1
547.	(x-7)(x-3)

548. x=7 and x=3
549. (x+11)(x+4)
550. x=-11 and x=-4
551. (x-9)(x-6)
552. x=9 and x=6
553. (x+12)(x+2)
554. x=-12 and x=-2
555. (x-12)(x-3)
556. x=12 and x=3
557. (x+9)(x+1)
558. x=-9 and x=-1
559. (x-11)(x-3)
560. x=11 and x=3
561. $(x+5)^2$
562. x=-5
563. (x-13)(x-2)
564. x=13 and x=2
565. (x+14)(x+3)
566. x=-14 and x=-3
567. (x-10)(x-7)
568. x=10 and x=7
569. (x+11)(x+11)
570. x = -11
571. (2x+4) (x-5)
572. x=-2 and x=5
573. (3x + 4) (x+6)
574. x=-4/3 and x=-6
575. (4x + 2) (3x-7)
576. x=-1/2 and x=7/3
577. (-2x + 3) (x + 2)
578. x = 3/2 and x=-2
579. (3x+3) (3x-4)
580. x=-1 and x=4/3
581. (2x + 4) (2x-1)
582. x = -2 and x=1/2
583. (5x+ 2) (x+1)
584. x=-2/5 and x=-1
585. (3x+1)(x-1)
586. x = -1/3 and x=1
587. (3x+7) (x+ 10)
588. x = -7/3 and x=-10
589. (5x+4) (x-3)

590.	x=-4/5 and x=3
591.	(7x+ 4) (2x+2)
592.	x = -4/7 and x=-1
593.	(3x+7) (9x + 4)
594.	x = -7/3 and x = -4/9
595.	(8x+ 3) (2x + 9)
596.	x = -3/8 and x = -9/2
597.	(3x + 2) (4x -7)
598.	x= -2/3 and x= 7/4
599.	(4x+7) (4x-3)
600.	x = -7/4 and x=3/4
601.	(6x+ 3) (4x-9)
602.	x=-1/2 and x = 9/4

Expand

603.	$(6x^2 + 8x + 2)$
604.	x=-1/3 and x=-1
605.	check graphing calculator
606.	$(12x^2 + 20x + 8)$
607.	x = -1 and x = -2/3
608.	check graphing calculator
609.	$(6x^2 + 9x + 3)$
610.	x=-1 and x=-1/2
611.	check graphing calculator
612.	$(20x^2 + 3x - 2)$
613.	x=-2/5 and x=1/4
614.	check graphing calculator
615.	$(6x^2 - x - 12)$
616.	x=3/2 and x=-4/3
617.	check graphing calculator
618.	$(6x^2 + 25x + 25)$
619.	x=-5/3 and x=-5/2
620.	check graphing calculator
621.	$(12x^2 + 10x - 2)$
622.	x=1/6 and x=-1
623.	check graphing calculator
624.	$(12x^2 - x - 6)$
625.	x=3/4 and x=-2/3
626.	check graphing calculator
627.	$(6x^2 + 21x + 15)$
628.	x=-1 and x=-5/2

629. check graphing calculator
630. $(12x^2 - 27x + 15)$
631. $x=5/4$ and $x=1$
632. check graphing calculator
633. $(15x^2 + x - 6)$
634. $x=3/5$ and $x=-2/3$
635. check graphing calculator
636. $(6x^2 + 38x + 56)$
637. $x=-7/3$ and $x=-4$
638. check graphing calculator
639. $(6x^2 + 10x - 4)$
640. $x=1/3$ and $x=-2$
641. check graphing calculator
642. $(x^2 - x - 20)$
643. $x=-4$ and $x=5$
644. check graphing calculator
645. $(x^2 + 4x + 3)$
646. $x=-3$ and $x=-1$
647. check graphing calculator
648. $(x^2 + 15x + 56)$
649. $x=-7$ and $x=-8$
650. check graphing calculator
651. $(2x^2 - 7x - 15)$
652. $x=-3/2$ and $x=5$
653. check graphing calculator
654. $(3x^2 - 11x - 4)$
655. $x=-1/3$ and $x=4$
656. check graphing calculator
657. $(6x^2 - x - 2)$
658. $x=-1/2$ and $x=2/3$
659. check graphing calculator
660. $(20x^2 + 11x - 4)$
661. $x=-4/5$ and $x=1/4$
662. check graphing calculator
663. $(3x^2 - x - 2)$
664. $x=-2/3$ and $x=1$
665. check graphing calculator
666. $(2x^2 - 19x - 10)$
667. $x=-1/2$ and $x=10$
668. check graphing calculator
669. $(6x^2 + 8x + 2)$
670. $x=-1/3$ and $x=-1$

671. check graphing calculator
672. (42x²+44x+10)
673. x=-5/7 and x=-1/3
674. check graphing calculator
675. (12x²+40x+32)
676. x=-4/5 and x=-2
677. check graphing calculator
678. (15x²+22x+8)
679. x=-4/5 and x=-2/3
680. check graphing calculator
681. (24x² + 26 + 6)
682. x=-3/4 and x=-1/3
683. check graphing calculator
684. (15x² +54x + 27)
685. x=-3 and x=-3/5
686. check graphing calculator
687. (56x²-17x-3)
688. x=-1/8 and x=3/7
689. check graphing calculator
690. (12x²-22x + 8)
691. x=1/2 and x=4/3
692. check graphing calculator
693. (2x²-x - 1)
694. x=-1/2 and x=1
695. check graphing calculator
696. (9x²+28x + 3)
697. x=-1/9 and x=-3
698. check graphing calculator
699. (6x²-12x-18)
700. x=-3 and x=-1
701. check graphing calculator
702. (20x²-35x+15)
703. x=1 and x=3/4
704. check graphing calculator
705. (16x²+ 20x+6)
706. x=-3/4 and x=-1/2
707. check graphing calculator
708. (6x²+31x+35)
709. x=-5/3 and x=-7/2
710. check graphing calculator
711. (18x²-24x+6)
712. x=1 and x=1/3

713.	check graphing calculator
714.	$(10x^2-17x-63)$
715.	$x=-9/5$ and $x=7/2$
716.	check graphing calculator
717.	$(40x^2+44x+12)$
718.	$-1/2$ and $x=-3/5$
719.	check graphing calculator
720.	$(6x^2-27x+30)$
721.	$x=5/2$ and $x=2$
722.	check graphing calculator
723.	$(28x^2+16x-12)$
724.	$x=-1$ and $x=3/7$
725.	check graphing calculator
726.	$(35x^2+26x-48)$
727.	$x=6/7$ and $x=-8/5$
728.	check graphing calculator
729.	$(6x^2+38x+40)$
730.	$x=5$ and $x=-4/3$
731.	check graphing calculator
732.	$(12x^2-7x-18)$
733.	$(x=3$ and $x=-1/2)$
734.	check graphing calculator
735.	$(4x^2+3x-1)$
736.	$(x=1/4$ and $x=-1)$
737.	check graphing calculator
738.	$(15x^2+17x-27)$
739.	$(x=9/5$ and $x=-7/3)$
740.	check graphing calculator
741.	$(7x^2+49x-56)$
742.	$(x=1$ and $x=-8)$
743.	check graphing calculator

Area Problems

744.	5
745.	6
746.	8
747.	11
748.	7
749.	2
750.	$\sqrt{5}$
751.	$3\sqrt{2}$

752.	√34
753.	3√3
754.	3√5
755.	2√21
756.	5√2
757.	√34
758.	2√21
759.	2√23
760.	√29
761.	√10
762.	6√2
763.	2√23
764.	6
765.	√31
766.	√97
767.	√70
768.	√73
769.	√29
770.	√94
771.	√82
772.	2√21
773.	3√10
774.	√15
775.	20
776.	5
777.	100pi
778.	25
779.	50
780.	15
781.	100pi
782.	225pi
783.	625pi
784.	1225pi
785.	676pi
786.	2025pi
787.	100pi
788.	81pi
789.	196pi
790.	324pi
791.	289pi
792.	25pi
793.	14pi

794. 82.6875
795. 9x2
796. (2√10 + 5) x (4√10 − 7)
797. 6
798. 9
799. 38/3
800. 83/9
801. 94/3
802. 4
803. 20/9
804. 37/6
805. 29/18
806. 15/8
807. 5
808. 8
809. 4
810. 5
811. 5√5
812. √77
813. 3√10
814. √73
815. 5√2
816. √58
817. 5
818. 10
819. 13
820. √65
821. √181
822. √170
823. √850
824. 5
825. 8
826. √149

Absolute Value

827. 45
828. 98
829. 24
830. 5
831. 7

832.	10
833.	2
834.	10
835.	2
836.	1
837.	4
838.	3
839.	2
840.	5
841.	3
842.	7
843.	92
844.	9
845.	3
846.	10
847.	5
848.	2
849.	1
850.	7
851.	11
852.	9
853.	7
854.	17
855.	12
856.	7
857.	2
858.	3
859.	4
860.	1
861.	3
862.	1
863.	4
864.	0
865.	3
866.	1
867.	0

www.ingramcontent.com/pod-product-compliance
Lightning Source LLC
Chambersburg PA
CBHW051727170526
45167CB00002B/833